Reconciling Faith and Reason

Apologists, Evangelists, and Theologians in a Divided Church

Thomas P. Rausch, S.J.

D1453426

A Michael Glazier Book
THE LITURGICAL PRESS
Collegeville, Minnesota

To

Raymond E. Brown, S.S.

In memoriam

A Michael Glazier Book published by The Liturgical Press

Cover design by David Manahan, O.S.B. Illustration: Abbey Archives.

Chapter 1 of this book was originally published as "Divisions, Dialogue, and the Catholicity of the Church" in the Jan. 31, 1998, issue of America. Reprinted with permission of America Press, Inc. © 1998 All Rights Reserved. For subscription information, call 1-800-627-9533 or visit www.americapress.org.

1   2   3   4   5   6   7   8

Library of Congress Cataloging-in-Publication Data

Rausch, Thomas P.
    Reconciling faith and reason : apologists, evangelists, and theologians in a divided church / Thomas P. Rausch.
        p. cm.
    "A Michael Glazier book."
    Includes bibliographical references and index.
    ISBN 0-8146-5956-X 9 (perfect bound).—ISBN 0-8146-5096-1 (case bound).
    1. Church controversies—Catholic Church. 2. Catholic Church—Doctrines.
I. Title.

BX1795.C69 R38 2000
282'.09'049—dc21

99-057872

Contents

Abbreviations   v

Introduction   vii

1. A Divided Church   1

    The Catholic Left   2
    The Conservative Catholic Subculture   5
    Conclusions   9

2. Contemporary Catholic Theology   11

    The Emergence of a Critical Theology   12
    Disputed Questions   20
    Conclusions   32

3. The New Apologists   35

    Apologetics   36
    The New Apologists   39
    Why Catholics Leave the Church   48
    Conclusions   50

4. Scripture, Tradition, and Church   53

    Tradition   54
    Scripture   56
    Church   62
    Conclusions   69

5. Sexual Morality   71

   Moral Theology   72
   A Practical Example   74
   Towards a More Biblical Morality   76
   Integrating Law and Gospel   80
   Conclusions   84

6. Eucharist and Liturgy   87

   Medieval Developments   89
   Vatican II and Liturgical Renewal   91
   Where We Are Today   93
   Unresolved Issues   95
   Conclusions   97

7. A New Evangelization   99

   Finding the Language that Gives Life   102
   Towards an Evangelical Theology   109
   Conclusions   113

8. Towards Common Ground in Theology   115

   Principles   117
   Conclusions   125

Index of Names   127

Index of Subjects   131

Abbreviations

Documents of Vatican II

DH   *Dignitatis humanae:* Declaration on Religious Freedom
DV   *Dei verbum:* Dogmatic Constitution on Divine Revelation
GS   *Gaudium et spes:* Pastoral Constitution on the Church in the Modern World
LG   *Lumen gentium:* Dogmatic Constitution on the Church
NA   *Nostra aetate:* Declaration on the Relationship of the Church to Non-Christian Religions
OT   *Optatem totius:* Decree on Priestly Formation
SC   *Sacrosanctum concilium:* Constitution on the Sacred Liturgy
UR   *Unitatis redintegratio:* Decree on Ecumenism

Other

BEM   World Council of Churches, *Baptism, Eucharist and Ministry* (WCC: Geneva, 1982).
CDF   Congregation for the Doctrine of the Faith
DS   Denzinger-Schönmetzer, *Enchiridion Symbolorum* 33rd ed. (Freiburg: Herder, 1965).
WCC   World Council of Churches

Introduction

One of the leading Catholic theologians in the years before the Second Vatican Council was the French Jesuit, Jean Daniélou. A patristics scholar and professor at the *Institut Catholique* in Paris, he and fellow Jesuit Henri de Lubac founded and edited the *Sources Chrétiennes,* a critical edition of the works of the Church Fathers. Both were leaders in the movement known as the "new theology," an effort of scholars particularly in France to return to the biblical, patristic, and liturgical sources which had so enriched the self-understanding of the Church of the first millennium. Like many of these scholars who were challenging the textbook theology of the Roman schools, Daniélou came under suspicion for some of his work. But he was ultimately vindicated; he served as a *peritus* or expert at Vatican II and was consulted for the pastoral constitution on the Church in the Modern World. Of particular interest for him were the relations between Christianity and culture. Pope Paul VI named him a cardinal in 1969.

In his later years Daniélou became concerned about the direction of the post-conciliar Church and the work of a new generation of Catholic theologians. He became quite polemical, denouncing theologians for their pedantry, their efforts to dilute papal authority, to introduce democracy into the Church. One of his essays appeared recently on a traditionalist Catholic Internet site.[1] To read his comments on baptism and its relation to original sin, the doctrine of the Real Presence, the question of its presence in other traditions, the theory of the anonymous Christian, or what he sees as the efforts to "politicize" the Church, is not just to recognize

---

1. Jean Daniélou, "I am in the Church," at http://praiseofglory.alabanza.com/jdanielou.htm.

the positions of theologians with whom he disagrees. It is also to recognize his fear for the Church he loves. Though one might agree with this point or that, much of what he wrote was overstated. Reading it today from the perspective of twenty-five years, he seems out of touch. But at bottom, Daniélou's essay is a cry from the heart from a theologian who had served the Church well and then saw theology move in directions he had not anticipated.

How sad it is, that scholars whose theological work did so much to prepare for the Second Vatican Council and found expression in its documents should feel betrayed by the efforts of other theologians who came after them, inspired in part by their example. Daniélou died in 1974. He would have had much more to complain about, had he lived longer. For there are serious divisions in the Catholic Church today. Some of them are theological: the nature of theology and what counts as evidence, the extent of revelation, the relation between theology and church authority, reason and faith, and the issue of whose voices are to be heard in the development and formulation of doctrine. Some are theoretical questions such as different understandings of what constitutes divine law or divine institution and what is merely culturally conditioned historical development. Some are more practical: questions concerning biblical interpretation, sexuality, liturgy, the role of women in the Church, and different approaches to catechesis, religious education, and evangelization. But they divide Catholics from one and other, with people of good will and a profound commitment to the Church on both sides.

In the pages that follow I would like to explore in greater depth some of these divisions, the causes that underlie them, and their implications for the life of the Church. How can progressives and traditionalists, apologists and theologians, evangelists, catechists, and social activists learn to find the truth in the positions of the other? How can faith be reconciled with critical reason and the understanding of our world that comes from contemporary science? Can we identify some principles that might help us discover some common ground in the task of theology?

Throughout its long history Catholicism has been committed to the principle of the complementarity of faith and reason. It rejects any concept of double truth, one of reason, a different one of faith. The act of faith is itself reasonable. Reason is able to arrive at the truth of God's existence from the reflection of God in nature (cf. Rom 1:20); we can know *that* God is. Faith tells us *who* God is; it enables us to grasp the divine self-revelation. Thus reason is able to ground the act of faith and enable us to obtain a deeper understanding of faith's mysteries. The natural law tradition in Catholic moral theology reflects this confidence in the complementarity of faith and reason as does the Church's contemporary embrace of historical critical biblical scholarship.

With the emergence of modern science at the beginning of the modern period, the tension between faith and reason appeared in what frequently became the opposition between science and theology. This led occasionally to great embarrassments for the Catholic Church. The condemnation of Galileo in the seventeenth century is perhaps the most obvious example, but there have been others. The Church was slow to accept the heliocentric system of Copernicus and the theory of evolution. Pope Pius XII's encyclical *Humani generis* held Catholics to the belief that humankind evolved from a single set of parents, though this is a scientific question, not a theological one. And the Church has continued to show little interest in what can be learned from the social sciences.

Pope John Paul II's 1998 encyclical *Fides et ratio* is a strong reaffirmation of the compatibility of faith and reason.[2] The Pope stresses that revelation remains "charged with mystery," that our vision of God "is always fragmentary and impaired by the limits of our language" (no. 13). Reason has an important role in helping us to understand the mystery. John Paul repeats Anselm's "I believe in order to understand" *(credo ut intellegam)*. But he also turns Anselm's saying around, entitling chapter three *"Intellego ut Credam,"* I understand that I may believe. Here he shows his profound conviction as a philosopher in the compatibility of faith and reason. The two stand together in harmony, "without compromising their mutual autonomy" (no. 48).

The Pope also reminds us that the magisterium has rejected "fideism" and "radical traditionalism" as well as "rationalism" and "ontologism" (no. 52). He warns of "a resurgence of fideism, which fails to recognize the importance of rational knowledge and philosophical discourse for the understanding of faith, indeed for the very possibility of belief in God." One symptom of this fideism is a tendency towards a "biblicism" which appeals to the bible as the sole criterion of truth, thus eliminating the role of the Church. Another is the neglect of speculative theology and classical philosophy (no. 55).

Pope John Paul's emphasis on reason and faith working in consort establishes the context for this book. The first chapter surveys the divisions in the contemporary Catholic Church.

Chapter 2 traces the emergence and development of a renewed, declericalized, but often overly academic Catholic theology. This theology has benefited the Church enormously, but in its independence it has

---

2. John Paul II, *Fides et Ratio. Origins* 28 (1998) 317–47.

sometimes moved into an adversarial position vis-à-vis the Church, not just critiquing the tradition, but occasionally moving beyond it.

Chapter 3 focuses on the new apologists as a conservative reaction to the excesses of academic theology as well as to the changing nature of the Church. Critical theology and the new apologists are opposed here as practical examples; they are not polar opposites. Neither fully represents its respective "wing." There are expressions of liberal Catholicism that are neither theological nor responsible. And there are many expressions of the Catholic right which lack the pastoral and evangelical concerns of the new apologists. I have contrasted them with the theologians of the academy because what they share in common is an interest in theology, though their approaches and concerns are very different.

Chapter 4, on Scripture, tradition, and the Church, explores the relation of Scripture and tradition. Then it asks, what does it mean to say that the Catholic tradition is a living tradition, able to develop, to face new questions, even to change.

Chapter 5 considers the question of the Church and sexuality. It contrasts traditional moral theology with the approach known as proportionalism, looks at the debate over homosexuality as a test case, and tries to move towards a sexual ethic that balances the traditional approach with a greater reliance on the biblical tradition.

Chapter 6 is on liturgy and Eucharist. In the context of the present controversy over what is appropriate for the Church's liturgical life, it reviews some unhappy developments in the medieval Church as well as the principles of liturgical reform articulated by Vatican II. Then it looks at the lights and shadows in contemporary Catholic liturgical practice and at some unresolved issues which continue to divide Catholics.

Chapter 7, written in response to Pope John Paul II's call for a new evangelization, raises the question, how do we find an evangelical, theological language that gives life? It assesses various efforts to express the Church's evangelical mission, both traditional and contemporary, and then seeks to sketch the assumptions and concerns that ought to characterize a contemporary evangelical theology.

The final chapter attempts to lift up some principles for doing theology in a divided Church. How can we find "common ground," doing theology in a way that is at once critical, evangelical, and faithful to the Catholic tradition? This is the fundamental concern of this book.

I am deeply grateful to Michael Downey, longtime colleague and friend, for his wise counsel as I was preparing the manuscript for this book. For what in the end it says, the responsibility is my own.

1

A Divided Church

Who is not aware of the divisions in our Catholic community. I was reminded of this recently as I was preparing to preside at a Mass for an assembly of women religious. Before the liturgy began, I was given a script for the prayers which it was clear I was to follow. Carefully banished from the text were the words "Father," "Lord," and "kingdom." The blessing at the end was not the traditional trinitarian formula but an inclusive invocation: "May our God, Creator, Redeemer, and Life-giving Spirit bless us." I am in favor of inclusive language. But one needs to move very carefully when dealing with the historic symbols of our faith. By predicating Creator, Redeemer, and Life-giving Spirit of God and by eliminating (however inadvertently) the mutual relationship between Father and Son, this formula seems to eliminate the distinction of persons, and thus, the doctrine of the Trinity. Even more, it depersonalizes God.

Despite my misgivings about the text, it obviously represented a pastoral effort to pray in a more inclusive fashion, one that moved beyond the androcentric character of so much of our God-language. But other examples are more extreme. In a recent issue of the *National Catholic Reporter,* there was a story of a eucharistic ritual called "A Critical Mass" which took place in Oakland, California. It opened with a priest in traditional vestments processing into the assembly and then intoning, "In the name of the Father . . ." at which point a horn was blown and dancers emerged, a sign that the priest should make his exit so that all those gathered could take over the service.[1] This was an extreme example, but as one of the organizers said, similar women's liturgies with non-ordained presiders are being celebrated across the country and around the world.

1. *National Catholic Reporter* 33/44 (17 October 1997) 4.

1

In another, very difficult case, Bishop Matthew Clark in 1998 dismissed Rev. James Callan as pastoral administrator of Corpus Christi Parish in Rochester, New York. Callan had allowed women to minister at the altar in ways that appeared "priestly," blessed gay and lesbian unions, and invited those of other faith traditions to receive Communion, all actions against current church discipline. In 1999 about two hundred members of Corpus Christi separated from the parish and established a "New Faith Community" no longer in communion with the bishop, with Callan as their pastor.

One could list an equal number of examples of hardened attitudes, separatist practices, actions against the communion of the Church from the right. We have on our campus some very conservative Catholic students, instructed by some even more conservative faculty members, who will not serve at Mass as lectors or eucharistic ministers—because "that is what priests are suppose to do." This sounds very much like the neo-clericalism of Opus Dei. It is clearly contrary to what the liturgical norms allow. One professor encouraged a student in the campus ministry RCIA program to join instead another one at a parish which regularly offered the Tridentine Mass. On another Jesuit campus, students belonging to a very conservative institute were accustomed to attend campus ministry liturgies, not to worship but to report liturgical infractions; now they have their own liturgies with their priest advisors.

We all have our collections of anecdotes, from both sides. But beyond these, there are serious problems, groups and movements whose members are increasingly locked into angry, no-compromise positions. There are many today who are openly contemptuous of magisterial and particularly papal authority. Others reject the leadership of the American bishops and appeal over their heads to Rome. What is at risk is the life of the church community itself as a community of faith, love, and service.

The Catholic Left

The Catholic left consists of a broad spectrum of positions, movements, and theologies. Some are progressive, seeking to continue and deepen in the life of the Church what they understand as the renewal begun by the Second Vatican Council (1962–1965). Taking theology seriously, they have both contributed to and benefited from its renewal in the Church. They represent a critical reappropriation of the tradition. Others, more radical, challenge the received tradition in fundamental ways. Some show little appreciation for sustained theological reflection. Like their counterparts on the right, they are driven by personal or ideological issues. Whether on the right or the left, these groups are pragmatic in orientation, little concerned for either careful reflection on the tradition or speculative theology.

On the left are an increasing number of advocacy groups working for change. Dignity, an organization for gay and lesbian Catholics, works for the full integration of homosexuals in the Church, including the acceptance of their sexual relations. Corpus advocates the return of former priests to active ministry. The Women's Ordination Conference, Call To Action, We Are the Church, Priests for Equality, National Coalition of American Nuns, Catholics for Free Choice—all are movements pushing for change, often in ways that directly challenge church teaching and ecclesiastical authority.

Perhaps more serious is the growing chasm between professional theology and the life and faith of the Church. In an article tracing the development of theology as a professional discipline in Catholic universities, Marquette's Patrick Carey shows how Catholic theology after Vatican II became increasingly academic, moving away from the moral and pastoral concerns which had earlier characterized the discipline. By 1967, when the Society of Catholic College Teachers of Sacred Doctrine changed its name to the College Theology Society, Carey writes that a concern for the religious lives of the students had become "an obsolete relic of a now defunct system."[2] His conclusion calls for a rethinking of the task of college theology in order to address issues such as the intellectualism in the discipline that ignores the religious development of the person, the ignored or lost Catholic identity of many departments, and the religious illiteracy of so many college students.

The problems Carey speaks of are very real. The contextual emphasis in contemporary scholarship has led to increasingly specialized theologies—liberation, feminist, and ecological—focusing on the interests of particular disadvantaged groups. Feminist theology, for example, has been subdivided into feminist, "womanist," and *mujerista* theology (for white middle class, African-American, and Hispanic women respectively). Influenced by postmodernism, these contextual theologies tend to regard all knowledge as politically constructed on the basis of power, gender, ethnicity, and social status. In order to address current issues in Church and society, they frequently reinterpret or "deconstruct" the tradition, substituting new orthodoxies and sometimes alternative histories. Many of these

---

2. Patrick W. Carey, "College Theology in Historical Perspective," in *American Catholic Traditions: Resources for Renewal,* ed. Sandra Yocum Mize and William Portier (New York: Orbis, 1997) 262.

theologies seem more ideological than evangelical or religious. It is not at all clear that they are able or even interested in leading others to that personal relationship with God in Christ called for by Pope John Paul II in his 1990 encyclical on evangelization, *Redemptoris missio* (no. 44).

Thus conservative Catholics do not trust the theology of the academy; they object that it has demythologized the Bible into meaningful stories rather than narratives that have something to do with history, deconstructed the authority of the Church and its ordained ministry, substituted a permissive sexual ethics for traditional Catholic morality, and transformed Catholic theology into the ideological agenda of contemporary liberal culture. They warn about the loss of a sense for the sacred, and long for the dignity of the old Latin Mass. And they rightly point to the theological illiteracy and ignorance of the Catholic tradition of so many young Catholics.

Nor are such critics simply exaggerating. They have some legitimate concerns. The fact that so many Catholic university students are unable to summarize the message of the Gospel in concrete terms or to explain the meaning of the creed seems to confirm their negative judgment. Recently I had three first-year Catholic students say on their final papers that they appreciated working through the biblical and theological foundations of the Eucharist because they had not been aware of the doctrine of the real presence. I have found a similar ignorance of basic doctrines in other classes. Yet in many lower-division classes Catholic students are introduced to all the controverted areas of contemporary theology and shown how to deconstruct contested positions before they are really familiar with the tradition out of which they are supposed to address these questions.

The problem of theological illiteracy and ignorance of the Catholic tradition among young Catholics is very real, and the theological academy is not without some responsibility. For example, I recently came across a professor's book list for first-year students at a Catholic university which recommended books by John Dominic Crossan and Robert Funk in christology as well as Uta Ranke-Heinemann and Bishop John Shelby Spong in ecclesiology. Even though some of these authors are Catholic in background, none could be considered even remotely sympathetic to the Church, nor could I find more mainstream authors on his bibliography.

Richard McBrien likes to point out, correctly, that theology is different from catechesis. In his own work, McBrien is careful to develop the religious side of the discipline. But there are too many members of the theological academy who seem less interested in theology as faith seeking understanding. As Baptist theologian Timothy George has said, "Theologians are not freelance scholars of religion, but trustees of the deposit of faith that they, like pastors, are charged with passing on intact to the rising generation."[3] When young adult Catholics are so poorly instructed in the basics of their faith, those teaching theology in Catholic universities cannot ignore the kerygmatic and religious dimensions of their discipline.

On the other hand, the answer is not to be found by turning to the theology of the Catholic right wing which too often approaches church teaching with little heed to questions of interpretation, is unable to recognize development or change, and presupposes a monarchical ecclesiology. Such theology offers certainty at the price of real biblical and historical foundation, a perfect example of what Michael Novak once called "non-historical orthodoxy." In more contemporary terms, it represents a "Catholic fundamentalism," a fundamentalism of the magisterial document rather than of the biblical text.

The Conservative Catholic Subculture

Catholic conservatism is by no means homogeneous. As Michael Cuneo has shown in his fascinating book *The Smoke of Satan,* the Catholic right in the U.S. consists of a vast subculture of conservatives, neoconservatives, various Marian cults centered on apparitions of Mary, often accompanied by apocalyptic messages of impending doom, single issue anti-abortion activists, and separatists who are in fact in schism.[4]

The mainstream Catholic conservative movement represents an ultramontane position, a magisterial maximalism which sees all questions in the contemporary Church as resolvable simply by appealing to the papal magisterium. For this group, acceptance of *Humanae vitae,* Pope Paul VI's 1968 encyclical on human life which rules out contraception, is the touchstone of orthodoxy. Representatives include *The Wanderer,* an archconservative Catholic newspaper founded in 1867 for German immigrants, Catholics United for the Faith (CUF), founded in 1968 by H. Lyman Stebbins, a convert to Catholicism, the Fellowship of Catholic Scholars, a society for conservative Catholic academics founded in 1977 by Msgr. George A. Kelly which finds the work of even careful mainstream scholars like Raymond Brown and Avery Dulles dangerous,[5] and Hellen Hull Hitchcock's

---

3. Timothy George, "A Theology to Die For," *Christianity Today* 42/2 (1998) 49.

4. Michael W. Cuneo, *The Smoke of Satan: Conservative and Traditionalist Dissent in Contemporary American Catholicism* (New York/Oxford: Oxford University Press, 1997).

5. See James Hitchcock, "The Fellowship of Catholic Scholars," in *Being Right: Conservative Catholics in America,* ed. Mary Jo Weaver and R. Scott Appleby (Bloomington, Ind.: Indiana University Press, 1995) 192–93.

"Women for Faith and Family," founded in 1984. On the extreme edge of mainline conservatives one could add *Fidelity* magazine, founded in 1981 by E. Michael Jones.

There are also some more recent groups and movements such as Mother Angelica's Eternal Word Television Network (EWTN), a new group of Catholic apologists, several new, conservative Catholic colleges such as the Franciscan University of Steubenville (Ohio), Christendom College (Front Royal, Virginia), and Thomas Aquinas College (Santa Paula, California), a strong "home schooling" movement, as well as a number of new publications, advocacy groups, or mail order ministries. Many of these can be found on the Internet.

A second group, often described as "neoconservative," emerged in the late 1970s, usually identified with Michael Novak, Richard John Neuhaus, and George Weigel. A central concern of the neoconservatives is the defense of what Novak call "democratic capitalism," though they are also strong in their critique of feminism, abortion, and what is seen as the social agenda of the gay community. George Weigel describes them as taking up the challenge laid down by John Courtney Murray, S.J., "to devise a religiously grounded moral philosophy for the American experiment."[6]

The "new apologists," a group of Catholics popularizing a polemical apologetics that has much in common with Protestant fundamentalism, represents another new movement. One of the most popular of the new apologists is Karl Keating, the director of a lay organization called *Catholic Answers.* Keating publishes a monthly journal of apologetics, *This Rock,* designed to help Catholics counter the arguments of Protestant fundamentalists. Lately however, he claims to be turning his energies to those "dissenters and heretics within the Church" such as those in the "Call to Action" movement.[7]

The Catholic right has been quick to recognize the power of the Internet as a new medium for mass communication for an image oriented generation. A proliferation of sites maintained by both individuals and movements has become increasingly sophisticated, with multi-colored texts, clever graphics, photography and works of art, postings of church documents, the fathers, and essays by theologians and church officials, and hyperlinks to other sites. The Internet's ability to combine text with sound and visual imagery and the simultaneity of its information sites gives it an enormous power, affective as well as cognitive. While it has

6. George Weigel, "The Neoconservative Difference: A Proposal for the Renewal of Church and Society," in *Being Right,* 139.

7. *Catholic Answers* appeal letter (undated).

great potential for education and evangelization, too often, free of the constraints of scholarship or ecclesial sponsorship, it is ideologically driven. Thus it represents a new kind of "virtual" authority, based on technological competence.

Particularly troubling is the fact that many conservative Catholic groups skillfully exploit the differences between the U.S. bishops, trying to hold together a diverse and pluralistic church, and Rome.[8] *The Wanderer* regularly attacks bishops with whom they disagree, providing the addresses of Roman curial officials and encouraging their readers to write directly with their complaints. Catholics United for the Faith has also recommended the appeal to Rome. And an Illinois-based group, the "Roman Catholic Faithful," campaigns via the World Wide Web against "Bishops who are at war with Christ and His Holy Church."[9]

Joseph Fessio, S.J., founder of Ignatius Press, has gone to Rome in his battle against the U.S. bishops' efforts to introduce a moderate inclusive-language Lectionary. He urges a liturgical "reform of the reform" which recommends using only the first Eucharistic Prayer (the Roman canon), celebrating the Eucharist with the priest's back to the people, increased use of Gregorian chant and Latin, reinstalling communion rails, and limiting liturgical ministries to men and boys. Four separate articles in the November 1997 issue of his *Catholic World Report* took the bishops to task for their efforts at liturgical renewal, their struggle to develop a more inclusive liturgical language, for their pastoral letter "Always Our Children," reaching out to the parents of gay and lesbian Catholics, and for co-operating with professional societies such as the Catholic Theological Society of America, the Canon Law Society, and the Association of Catholic Colleges and Universities.

Another frequent critic of the bishops is Eternal Word Television Network's Mother Angelica. After Los Angeles Cardinal Roger Mahony wrote a pastoral letter on the Eucharist, Mother Angelica used her nationally syndicated program, "Mother Angelica Live," to accuse the cardinal of teaching that the eucharistic bread and wine remain unchanged. She expressed the hope that Catholics in the archdiocese would give him "zero" obedience.[10]

The intolerant and vituperative language in which disagreements are so often expressed makes real conversation very difficult. The *New Oxford*

---

8. See for example Rembert Weakland, "Liturgical Renewal: Two Latin Rites," *America* 176/20 (1997) 12–15.

9. Roman Catholic Faithful (http:/www.ref.org), 18 August 1997.

10. "Mother Angelica apologizes (sort of) for remarks about Cardinal Mahony," *The Tidings* (28 November 1997) 3.

Review regularly runs ugly advertisements with titles such as "Does Jesus Have Two Mommies?" or "Does St. Bozo's Parish No Longer Amuse You?" The ads refer to characters such as "Father Flake" and "Sister Shrew." *America* magazine has frequently had to apologize to its offended readers for carrying them and decided finally to ban these ads from all its publications, as did *Our Sunday Visitor.* The *New Oxford Review* responded to the latter by accusing its publishers of lacking "intestinal fortitude."[11]

On the West Coast, three ultraconservative papers, the *San Diego News Notes,* the *Los Angeles Lay Catholic Mission,* and *The Faith* in the San Francisco Bay area, all of them funded by a conservative Catholic publisher, have for some years attacked the Cardinal Archbishop of Los Angeles in particularly ugly terms. Criticizing the ministries and educational programs of the Archdiocese, particularly its ministry to gays and lesbians and its annual Religious Education Congress, the largest in the country, these papers well deserve the adjective "mean-spirited." One article, entitled "The Only Thing Missing Was the Golden Calf," attacked the closing liturgy at the 1996 Congress at which Cardinal Mahony presided, quoting two Congress observers who called it "pagan" and "blasphemous."[12]

Liberals can also be guilty of using intemperate or sarcastic language. Too often they ridicule Cardinal Ratzinger in highly personal terms, reduce the faith of conservative Catholics to a religion of law rather than love, and dismiss those uncomfortable with hand holding during the Lord's Prayer as not appreciating "community."[13]

The late Cardinal Joseph Bernardin's "Common Ground" initiative was an attempt to deal with the growing polarization that so often characterizes internal Catholic debates and fractures Catholic life. He wrote: "A mood of suspicion and acrimony hangs over many of those most active in the church's life; at moments it even seems to have infiltrated the ranks of bishops."[14] His initiative, proposed practically from his deathbed, was criticized by three of the U.S. cardinals.[15] Only Cardinal Mahony stood with Bernardin.

---

11. Dale Vree, *New Oxford Review* 65/2 (February 1998) 36.

12. *Los Angeles Catholic Mission,* April 1996.

13. See Frank Maguire, "Of common ground and long memories," *National Catholic Reporter* (3 July 1998) 25.

14. Joseph Bernardin, "Called to be Catholic: Church in a Time of Peril" *Origins* 26 (1996) 167.

15. See the excellent response by Kenneth E. Untener, "How Bishops Talk," *America* 175/11 (1996) 9–15.

Conclusions

Divisions in the Church is not a new phenomenon. St. Paul's First Letter to the Corinthians was written to a deeply divided community. The letter shows he was dealing with various factions or parties, people identifying themselves with Paul, Apollos, Peter, or Christ (1 Cor 1:12). When we look at them closely, it is interesting to see how contemporary this community seems.

We know that there were various theological approaches to the Gentile mission in the primitive Church, extending along a spectrum. At one extreme was a very conservative "traditionalist" approach that stressed full observance of the Mosaic Law. At the other was a radical Hellenistic group that saw no abiding significance in Jewish cults and feasts. The late Raymond Brown placed Peter on the less extreme side of the conservative group and Paul on the less radical side of the liberal group.[16]

Being aware of these differences in approach helps us better understand the divisions at Corinth. Those associated with Paul, the founder of the Church, would have followed his approach. Paul did not require Gentile converts to observe the Mosaic Law, but at the same time he did not prevent Jewish Christians from doing so. We can see those of the party of Paul as a more moderate or mainstream group, willing to accommodate what we would today call cultural difference. Those associated with Kephas, or Peter, would be the traditionalists; they would have argued for a more Law-observant expression of Christian life. Apollos, from Alexandria, was known as an eloquent preacher and probably for his worldly wisdom, judging from Paul's saying that he "did not come with sublimity of words or of wisdom" (1 Cor 2:1) and his emphasis on the very different wisdom of the gospel (1 Cor 2:2-13). Perhaps we could see those associated with Apollos as the more liberal intellectuals, the culturally sophisticated. Finally, there is the mysterious "Christ" party. Many scholars today see them as a gnostic group within the community who thought themselves as spiritually perfect and therefore above the law. It was most probably this group which threw back at Paul his own principle of Christian freedom in order to justify their lack of restraint in sexual matters (1 Cor 6:12-20). G. F. Synder suggests that they were members of a house church with gnostic leanings.[17] In this they would be like some house church groups today who authorize their own eucharistic practice.

---

16. Raymond E. Brown and John P. Meier, *Antioch and Rome* (New York: Paulist, 1983) 2–8.

17. Graydon F. Snyder, *First Corinthians* (Macon, Ga.: Mercer, 1992) 21–22.

What is important for our situation today is that with the exception of the man living in an incestuous relationship with his father's wife (1 Cor 5:1-5), Paul excommunicates no one at Corinth. Rather he urges and exhorts his difficult community, calling them back to his vision of their union as the body of Christ. The Church needs to be united for the sake of its mission. If we are to be faithful to that mission, we need to make a greater effort to understand each other. In the next chapter, we will consider the task of the theologians.

2

Contemporary Catholic Theology

The story of Catholic theology in the twentieth century is one of enormous development and change. Much of this story is positive. Having been freed from the shackles of an out-of-date method and from the repression that followed the Modernist crisis early in the century, Catholic theology has experienced a period of great creativity and fruitfulness. The achievements of the Second Vatican Council, expressed in its constitutions and decrees, is due in large part to the great work done by Catholic theologians in the decades immediately prior to the Council, though a number of them suffered for their efforts.

At the same time, the tension that always exists between theology as a work of the Church and theology as a critical discipline has at times resulted in an overly academic approach to theology which seems to have lost its foundation in the Church's life and faith. In the words of Avery Dulles: "Practically every doctrine that had been constitutive of Catholic orthodoxy has been contested by some prominent author. Papal infallibility, the Immaculate Conception of Mary, the Assumption of Mary, the virginal conception of Jesus, his bodily resurrection, the divinity of Christ, and the Trinity itself were either denied or radically reinterpreted to mean what they had never before been thought to mean."[1] What has happened, that someone of the stature of Dulles could make such a charge? To answer this, we need to take an overview of Catholic theology in the twentieth

1. Avery Dulles, *The Craft of Theology: From Symbol to System* (New York: Crossroad, 1996) ix.

11

century. We will review the emergence of theology as a critical discipline and its contribution to the life of the Church. Then we will look at a number of disputed issues, questions which have challenged and developed the tradition, but which also have contributed to the increasing polarization of the Church.

The Emergence of a Critical Theology

Catholic theology in the twentieth century has undergone a number of significant shifts which have reshaped it as a discipline. One was the shift from a "classicist" way of understanding to one based on historical consciousness. Another was the declericalization of theology in the period after the Second Vatican Council. This along with the increasing professionalization of the discipline resulted in a much more independent, critical theology which not infrequently has stood in some tension with the Church.

From Classicist to Historical Consciousness

In the mid-twentieth century Catholic theology underwent a profound shift which Bernard Lonergan has described as a transition from a classicist world view to one based on historical consciousness.[2] Prior to the Second Vatican Council Catholic theology understood its role as expounding and clarifying the divine truth taught by the magisterium. Its neoscholastic approach was largely speculative and deductive, rather than investigative. This "classicist" way of thinking was static rather than dynamic, proceeding from the abstract or universal to the particular case. Thus it stressed a perennial philosophy, absolute laws, and perfect definitions.

Catholic theology had not always been so unsympathetic to critical consciousness or scientific ways of thinking. At its best, it has rejected any split between reason and faith. St. Anselm (d. 1109) described theology as *fides quarens intellectum,* faith seeking understanding. Thus, reason has an important role to play in the task of theology. Thomas Aquinas emphasized that there can be no "double truth," a truth of faith at odds with the truth of reason. In his *Summa Contra Gentiles* he rejected a theological approach that relied on faith alone: "They hold a plainly false opinion who say that in regard to the truth of religion it does not matter what a person thinks about creation so long as he has the correct opinion concerning God. An error concerning the creation ends in false thinking about God" (*CG,* 2,3).

2. Bernard J. F. Lonergan, "The Transition from a Classicist World View to Historical Mindedness," *A Second Collection,* eds. William F. J. Ryan and Bernard J. Tyrrell (London: Darton, Longman and Todd, 1974) 1–9.

Yet in the period after the Reformation, Catholic theology became increasingly deductive, defensive and apologetic. In the effort to justify Catholic doctrine against the Reformers, authority became more and more important as a theological source while Rome itself became increasingly authoritarian. Pope Paul III established the old inquisition as a Roman congregation in 1542. The Index of Forbidden Books, forbidding Catholics to read or even possess certain authors, was established in 1557 by Paul IV. In the following period, theologians appealed to the authority of the doctrinal tradition, carefully watched over by Rome, rather than to the sources of that tradition. Though nineteenth-century theologians like John Henry Newman in England and those connected with the Tübingen School in Germany regularly used historical scholarship in their work, the Roman reaction to what was perceived as the threat of Modernism in the early part of the twentieth century led to an even more repressive period which was to exact a heavy price on Catholic scholarship.

Pope Pius X's encyclical *Pascendi* and the Holy Office's decree *Lamentabili* (both 1907) were followed by a fifty-year period marked by suspicion and repression. Seminary professors and even bishops were required to take annually the oaths against Modernism. The neoscholastic theology of the Roman schools, taught from Latin manuals, became the norm. Scripture and tradition were used "as an armory of authoritative statements to clarify and defend the teachings of the Church."[3] Theology that did not conform to this model was suspect; scholars were not infrequently dismissed from their positions or had their books placed on the Index. The attitude towards Protestant theology or modern intellectual movements was generally negative. In the Roman view, the role of theology was to analyze and clarify the divine truth taught by the magisterium. As late as 1950, Pope Pius XII wrote in his encyclical *Humani generis* that the proper task of theologians was "to indicate for what reasons those things which are taught by the living magisterium are found in Holy Scripture and divine 'tradition,' whether explicitly or implicitly" (DS 3886).[4] Thus the model for Catholic theology was a Roman theology based not on research or historical study of the received tradition, but on authority; it was largely deductive and speculative, expressed in the categories of scholastic philosophy.

---

3. Dulles, *The Craft of Theology,* 23; see also "The Problem of Method: From Scholasticism to Models," 41–52.

4. See Yves Congar, "A Brief History of the Magisterium and Its Relations with Scholars," *The Magisterium and Morality,* ed. Charles E. Curran and Richard A. McCormick, vol. 3 (New York/Ramsey: Paulist, 1982) 325.

There were some signs of hope. The most positive development in the period between 1920 and 1960 has been described by the French word *ressourcement,* "return," meaning a return to the sources of Catholic theology in Scripture, the Fathers of the Church, and the liturgy. Out of this came the acceptance by Catholic scholars of the modern biblical movement, the liturgical movement, and particularly in France, a movement known as the "new theology" *(nouvelle théologie).* Yet many of those who attempted to use these new methods in their work suffered for it. Scholars such as Karl Rahner, Yves Congar, Henri de Lubac, Marie-Dominique Chenu, Teilhard de Chardin, and the American Jesuit John Courtney Murray were either silenced, forbidden to write on certain topics, or disciplined, though their work would later shape the documents of Vatican II.[5]

The Church gradually came to accept historical critical scholarship, greatly helped by three great encyclicals of Pius XII: *Divino Afflante Spiritu* (1943) embracing modern biblical criticism, *Mystici Corporis* (1943) on the Church as the body of Christ, and *Mediator Dei* (1947) on the liturgy, with its guarded embrace of the liturgical movement. The result was that a major shift took place. Rather than being a deductive and apologetic discipline, a new, more critical theology began to emerge, reexamining the sources of Catholic theology, investigating historical developments, reinterpreting traditional formulas, and turning increasingly towards experience. The old scholastic framework was abandoned. The abstract, dogmatic "classicist" way of understanding had given way to a new one, based on historical consciousness. Theology was becoming an interpretative and constructive discipline.

The Laicization of Theology

A second shift concerned *who* was doing theology. Prior to the council, the study of theology took place largely in seminaries; it was a clerical endeavor, taught by priests for seminarians. Undergraduate students in Catholic colleges and universities took courses in religion; they did not study theology. There were no graduate programs for women in theology in the United States until 1943, when Sr. Madeleva Wolff, C.S.C., began a School of Sacred Theology for women religious at St. Mary's College at Notre Dame, Indiana. In 1952 Pope Pius XII founded Regina Mundi, a pontifical institute in Rome, to prepare women for teaching theology in Catholic women's colleges. In 1963 Marquette University's Bernard Cooke established the first doctoral program open to lay men and women, though

---

5. See for example, Thomas O'Meara, "'Raid on the Dominicans': The Repression of 1954," *America* 170/4 (1994) 8–16.

the program was called "religious studies," to head off possible objections from Rome.

Other Catholic universities followed Marquette's lead. By the end of the 1960s, lay men and increasingly lay women began enrolling in these programs. As they completed their degrees and began moving into faculty positions, the locus of theology began to change, from the seminaries to universities and graduate schools, and it was being done increasingly by lay men and women rather than by priests and religious. In recognition of this, the Catholic Theological Society of America, originally an association of seminary professors, began admitting lay members in 1965.

The Professionalization of Academic Theology

The period from 1965 to the early 1970s saw considerable changes in the way that religion was taught on the college level. Prior to the council, undergraduates in Catholic colleges and universities took courses in religion, not theology. The primary concern was doctrinal orthodoxy and religious formation. The courses were taught by instructors who lacked the academic credentials increasingly expected in other departments, met fewer hours per week, and received less credit.

However in the decade following the council Catholic colleges and universities began to develop professional departments of theology or religious studies. Religious studies stressed the objective study of religion as a phenomenon; its approach was neutral, rather than rooted in a particular faith tradition. Theology still understood itself as faith seeking understanding. But as Patrick Carey says, both were strictly academic disciplines, moving away "from what some were now considering the outdated pastoral functions of the college discipline."[6]

As those colleges and universities revised their core curricula, the number of courses required in theology or religious studies was greatly reduced, from seven or eight classes to the present average of two, both of which are usually elective. Philosophy also underwent a similar reduction. And as the numbers of priests and religious declined, the number of lay men and women increased. They were competent theologians, well-trained, and subject to the same requirements for tenure and promotion as their colleagues in other departments; that is, they were expected to publish, and they brought before their students all the issues they were pursuing in their research. But they were academics; the majority of them had

---

6. See Patrick W. Carey, "College Theology in Historical Perspective," in *American Catholic Traditions: Resources for Renewal,* edited by Sandra Yocum Mize and William Portier (Maryknoll: Orbis, 1997) 261.

neither the pastoral responsibilities of their religious and clerical predecessors nor their long years of spiritual and religious formation. And because their professional home is the academy rather than the Church, their theology is most often done according to a strictly academic model. They do not always have the same commitment to the Church's doctrinal tradition and authority that one presumes for a theologian whose base is the Church.

The shifts we have been considering have resulted in a far more independent and critical Catholic theology done by men and women much less subject to ecclesiastical authority. Unlike their clerical predecessors, or priests like Hans Küng and Charles Curran who taught on pontifical or ecclesiastical faculties, they teach at semi-autonomous Catholic universities or graduate schools. These institutions are not under the local bishop's control, despite the continuing efforts of Rome to require these theologians to obtain a mandate or official approval from "competent ecclesiastical authority."[7] Other Catholic theologians teach at non-Catholic institutions.

While theology should always be a task of the Church, it no longer sees itself as simply finding reasons to support the teachings of the magisterium. Part of its task is to reinterpret the Church's language so that it might more adequately reflect the faith it is intended to express. Every "expression of revelation" is historically conditioned, and therefore capable of more adequate expression, as the Congregation for the Doctrine of the Faith acknowledged in its 1973 instruction *Mysterium ecclesiae*.[8] As it assists in this task of reinterpretation, Catholic theology today is far more independent than it was in the past when it was the work almost exclusively of priests and religious. Thus it should not be surprising that at times a tension develops between theologians and the magisterium.

Part of the tension results from the critical nature of theology. Theology is a *scientific* reflection on faith; it has a number of critical tasks or "specialities." Some theologians are involved in "hermeneutical" or interpretive studies to recover the historical meaning of the biblical texts. Some work to "retrieve" historical information about the period of Christian origins. Some analyze hidden assumptions, traditional practices, and unexamined positions for a deeper understanding of Christian life. Still others are engaged in constructive efforts to re-express the Church's faith and doctrine in a more contemporary language and idiom.

---

7. Canon 812; cf., "Ex Corde Ecclesiae" *Origins* 20 (1990) art. 4, no. 3.
8. "Declaration in Defense of the Catholic Doctrine on the Church Against Certain Errors of the Present Day," *Origins* 3 (1973) 97–100.

Biblical studies have given us a much greater appreciation of the complexity of the biblical tradition, and thus, a new insight into how God's revelation is mediated in history. We are comfortable in seeing the book of Isaiah as the compilation of the work of three prophetic figures active at different times in the history of Israel, and we recognize that the New Testament represents not one but many theologies. The rediscovery of Paul's vision of a multiplicity of gifts and ministries in the Christian community has led to a new appreciation of the variety of ministries in today's Church; we no longer use the term "ministry" exclusively for clergy. We have been able to recover the important role played by women in the primitive Christian communities, and we have seen how an accommodation to cultural conditions in the late New Testament period led to a loss of this richness.

From the Fathers of the Church we have begun to appreciate again the central place of the doctrine of the Trinity, and of the importance of the theology of the Holy Spirit. Historical studies have helped us to see that the Church's threefold ministry of bishops, presbyters, and deacons developed gradually from the variety of ministries in the primitive churches, and that ordination as a sacramental sign of appointment to office emerged in the later New Testament period. We have come to understand the Church of the first millennium as a communion of churches rather than as a single institution, and we have rediscovered the importance of the concept of communion (Greek *koinonia*) for the Church of today and tomorrow. Studies on the ecclesial practice of reception have helped us to appreciate better that the magisterium speaks *for* the Church, rather than *to* it. We have a greater appreciation of the issues at stake in the Reformation and of how close the traditions were in the sixteenth century.

Liturgical studies have allowed us to recover the ancient practice of Christian initiation which led to the present RCIA, one of the most successful and fruitful liturgical reforms of the council. We have rediscovered the variety of roles in the liturgical assembly, and the fact that it is the assembly itself that is the real celebrant of the liturgy. Recognizing changes in the history of the liturgy, for example, the efforts of various councils and synods to outlaw the "abuse" of private confession, introduced by the Irish monks in the sixth century and only gradually accepted by the Church, makes it easier to understand and accept changes in our liturgical practice today.

Systematic theology seeks to give a unified theological vision by showing how the basic doctrines of the faith are related to each other. It also investigates the religious realities which lie behind those doctrines. Liberation theologies and studies in spirituality have contributed to a new awareness that the life of faith is not just a message about the next life; it illumines, transforms, and gives new hope to *this* life.

Much has been accomplished through the theological renewal which followed the council. At the same time, the expectations raised by the council, the currents of renewal it unleashed, and the probings of a new and independent theology into questions long unaddressed or excluded from discussion heightened the tension between theology as a work of the Church and theology as a critical discipline. While these two aspects of theology are not incompatible, the tension sharpened as questions of authority, ministry, women in the Church, and sexuality increasingly emerged in the postconciliar Church. As theologians became more outspoken on these and other questions, the official Church reacted, defending its positions with various instructions, declarations, and decrees and disciplining or silencing dissenting theologians. The list of those who have come under suspicion or censure is a long one; it includes Jacques Pohier in France, Edward Schillebeeckx in Holland, Hans Küng, a Swiss professor at Tübingen, Jacques Dupuis in Rome, Leonardo Boff and Ivone Gebara in Brazil, Jose María Castillo, Juan Antonio Estrada, and Benjamin Forcano in Spain, Tissa Balasuriya in Sri Lanka, Anthony de Mello in India, as well as Charles Curran and Matthew Fox in the United States. These actions of Rome exacerbated the polarization sketched earlier.

Conservative Catholics, unsettled by change—in the culture of the Church, in attitudes towards authority, in religious education, particularly in the liturgy—tended to blame the new theology, or more specifically, the theologians. Unable to see the connection between their work and the faith as they themselves have understood it, they are enormously suspicious of much of contemporary theology. They see it as a purely academic exercise, secular rather than religious, captive to a liberal culture, no longer rooted in the life and faith of the Church. They fear that contemporary theology is more concerned with revising or even deconstructing the tradition than with transmitting it intact to the next generation.

And in some ways they are correct. There is all too often a split between the theology of the academy and the pastoral life of the Church, the result at least in part of the professionalization of theology in the period following the council. Catherine Mowry LaCugna has argued that the Church itself is at least in part responsible for this split between theology and the Church's pastoral life. She observed that far more Catholic women pursue doctoral degrees in theology than women in Protestant churches, and that most feminist theologians are Catholics:

> The theologian is supposed to have one foot in the door of the academy, the other in the door of the church. In the past, theological work arose out of commentary on, and constant preaching of, Scripture. The present situation for Catholic theologians who are women means we are neither en-

couraged nor expected to acquire pastoral experience; or, if we do have pastoral experience, it is not recognized as a public ministry of the church. Further, most of us have few or no opportunities to test and sharpen theological insights through regular preaching. The irony, then, is that not ordaining women contributes to the serious breach between theology and pastoral practice.[9]

Are theologians today intent on a radical reinterpretation of Catholic faith, contesting every doctrine, deconstructing what they find objectionable in the tradition, pursuing the novel for its own sake? It is true that a certain amount of reinterpretation and reformulation is unavoidable as theology pursues its task of seeking greater understanding of the faith in light of the issues facing the contemporary Christian community. For example, LaCugna writes that feminist theology "almost always entails the commitment to promote the full humanity of women and men by critiquing, deconstructing, or reforming institutions or forms of thought that demean human persons."[10] But this is nothing new. The Church must always critique and renew its theological language. To deny this is to risk transforming the living tradition of the Church into a dead traditionalism.

One of the greatest strengths of Catholicism is precisely its teaching office, its magisterium, which allows the Church to reinterpret and occasionally to correct its tradition when confronted with new questions. The Catholic tradition is a living tradition, not a dead one. I've been reminded of this over and over again through contacts with Evangelical Protestants. Always fearful of the slippery slope leading to liberal Protestantism, with its confusing doctrinal pluralism, and without an effective teaching office which might address new questions, many of them remain locked into a biblical literalism, the product of a rather recent and ultimately confessional doctrine of biblical inerrancy.

Not every theological critique of a belief, practice, or tradition is an attack on the Catholic tradition itself, the tradition with a capital "T." As Jaroslav Pelikan has said, "Tradition is the living faith of the dead; traditionalism is the dead faith of the living."[11] Too many older Catholics today, nervous about change, uncritically identify the tradition with the Catholicism of their youth, a particular expression of the tradition deriving from the nineteenth and early twentieth century. For example, to suggest that

9. Catherine Mowry LaCugna, "Catholic Women as Ministers and Theologians," *America* 167 (1992) 248.

10. Catherine Mowry LaCugna, *God For Us: The Trinity and Christian Life* (San Francisco: HarperSanFrancisco, 1991) 268

11. Jaroslav Pelikan, *The Emergence of the Catholic Tradition (100–600)* (Chicago: University of Chicago Press, 1971) 9.

there is room in the Western Church for a married clergy, long the practice in the Eastern Church, is not to reject the tradition.

On the other hand, to someone who is not trained in the history and disciplines of theology, it could easily seem that what many Catholic theologians are saying today *is* destructive of the tradition, that they are indeed challenging established teachings, criticizing recent Vatican documents and positions, reinterpreting the nature of the Church, its sacraments, its moral teachings. Nor can it be denied that many theologians who identify themselves as Catholic no longer seem bound by the Church's doctrinal tradition. They reject teachings they disagree with, affirm more than the evidence will support in their work, sometimes even constructing alternative histories to support the reforms they advocate. One searches their writings for the love of the Church, including the official Church, that should distinguish sound theology, and finds instead only anger and rejection. Here questions of authority, sexuality, and, particularly, the place of women in the Church are the issues that focus the anger.

In the following section I would like to examine a number of areas where traditional theological positions are being challenged and rethought today. Much of this rethinking has been positive. Some of it has been more problematic, a radical reinterpretation or revision of the tradition rather than a fruitful reimagining of it. These are the controverted areas of contemporary theology, the *quaestiones disputatae* or disputed questions. We will consider God, christology, women in the Church, authority, as well as Eucharist and ministry. Sexuality will be taken up in a later chapter.

Disputed Questions

God

The Christian tradition has always recognized that God is both transcendent and immanent. As transcendent, God is the other, beyond our ability to grasp, to capture with our minds or express in our language. As immanent, God is near to us, reflected in nature, disclosed in symbols, present in the human heart. Yet the emphasis in much of contemporary theology is on a radical immanence; God is too easily identified with "whatever is human," experience becomes more important than biblical revelation," and the "otherness" of God risks being collapsed into a nature mysticism.

Feminist theology has raised the issue of how we name God, and is uncomfortable with speaking of God in our prayer and worship as though God were a male. One hears repeatedly Mary Daly's axiom, "if God is male, then the male is God."[12] Feminist theology seeks to find new ways to speak about God; its language is generally inclusive, relational, immanent, and inclined towards feminine metaphors. God has the tender and nurturing qualities of a mother. Her love is unconditional. Some feminists seek to reclaim and use the language of the "Goddess" in prayer.[13] They maintain that the experience of the Goddess reflects an original harmony; it is beyond dualism. The Goddess is seen, not as "other," but as a presence embracing opposites, healing and uniting.

In *She Who Is* Elizabeth Johnson reminds us that all our language about God is culturally conditioned. She notes that Christianity has traditionally spoken about God as though God were the ruling male within a patriarchal system. Even its most abstract concepts are dependent on a dualistic Greek philosophical tradition that equates the male principle with spirit, mind, reason, and act.[14] At the beginning of a brilliant chapter she asks, "Are human beings the holy ones who weep and groan, or can this also be predicated of the holy mystery of God who cherishes the beloved world?"[15] This of course is to challenge the traditional idea that God is all powerful, controlling all events.

Sallie McFague's work joins ecological to feminist concerns. Her book *Models of God* deals with immanental understandings of God as mother, lover, and friend of the world.[16] In *The Body of God* she examines a number of models in an effort to rethink God's transcendence in an immanent way. The deistic model imagines God as a clockmaker who winds up the world and lets it run according to its laws. This model has been popular with scientists but has the effect of distancing God from the world.

A dialogic model, popular with traditional Protestantism and with twentieth-century existentialism, reduces God's interaction with the world to the innersubjective relations of God and the individual. This moves beyond traditional supernaturalism, but ends up limiting God's relation to the world to inner human experience.

The monarchical model sees God as the all-powerful king who rules over his subjects and expects their service. But its emphasis on God's power does not adequately leave room for human freedom and limits God's

12. Mary Daly, *Beyond God the Father* (Boston: Beacon Press, 1973) 19.

13. Carol P. Christ, "Why Women Need the Goddess," *Womanspirit Rising,* ed. Judith Plaskow and Carol P. Christ (San Francisco: Harper & Row, 1979).

14. Elizabeth A. Johnson, *She Who Is: The Mystery of God in Feminist Discourse* (New York: Crossroad, 1992) 34–35.

15. Ibid., 246.

16. Sallie McFague, *Models of God: Theology for an Ecological, Nuclear Age* (Philadelphia: Fortress, 1987).

influence to the human sphere, rather than seeing God as the sustaining power and goal of the entire universe.

From the perspective of the "agential" model, the divine purpose is expressed in and through the world just as the self expresses itself through the body. Yet it tends to understand God as a super person directing the world and makes it difficult to distinguish divine acting from evolutionary history.

The final model, the organic, is pantheistic; it sees the universe as God's body but is unable to distinguish God from the world, and so does not recognize divine transcendence. McFague proposes a theology which combines the agential model with the organic. In this way, God becomes the spirit, the life and breath, of the world, while retaining for the divine a transcendence to the world.[17]

While McFague recognizes that our language about God is metaphorical, she speaks throughout her book of the world as the body of God. From this perspective, Jesus becomes the paradigmatic but not exclusive embodiment of God. She revises the traditional trinitarian formula, "The Father, the Son, and Holy Spirit," as "the mystery of God (the invisible face or first person), the physicality of God (the visible body or second person), and the mediation of the invisible and the visible (the spirit or third person). She argues that "the close association of the metaphors of father and son . . . undermines divine transcendence, since the biological or generational identification is implied."[18] But this risks collapsing the "immanent Trinity," the inner reality of God as a communion of persons, into the "economic Trinity," God as manifested in the history of salvation.

Joseph Bracken, while recognizing the metaphorical nature of terms such as "Father" and "Son," argues against the tendency in contemporary trinitarian theology to reject the immanent Trinity as idle speculation. He finds this "too radical in that it seems to set aside almost two thousand years of careful theological reflection on the reality of God as derived from Scripture and Tradition."[19] He proposes instead a shift from a metaphysics of being to a metaphysics of becoming, a metaphysics which sees relations as constituting the reality of things and being itself as intersubjective. Thus Bracken, using process philosophy, reaffirms the relationality which is at the heart of the Christian doctrine of the Trinity.

---

17. See Sallie McFague, *The Body of God: An Ecological Theology* (Minneapolis: Fortress, 1993) 137–41.

18. Ibid., 193.

19. Joseph A. Bracken, "Trinity: Economic *and* Immanent," *Horizons* 25/1 (1998) 8.

Christology

Jesus himself has undergone a radical reinterpretation, from his conception to his death and resurrection, in the work of contemporary theologians. Much of this has been very helpful, moving methodologically from a christology "from above," which starts from the doctrine of the Church, more appropriate for catechesis and preaching, to a christology "from below," which takes much more seriously the historical Jesus, his life and ministry, the resurrection, and the development of the gospel tradition. One finds this approach in theologians such as Walter Kasper, Edward Schillebeeckx, Raymond Brown, and John P. Meier.

Critical scholarship has forced a rethinking of the miracle tradition. Some miracle stories, for example, the "nature" miracles, may be just that; they are seen as stories, later additions to the Jesus tradition.[20] But the many reports, variously expressed, that Jesus cured the sick and even raised the dead fulfill the biblical criterion of multiple attestation, suggesting that these traditions are indisputably rooted in the gospel tradition. How to *interpret* miracles is another question. Many Catholic scholars are reluctant to describe them as "interventions" which suspend the laws of nature; this is only one possible explanation, and violates the principle of the complementarity of faith and reason. Another way of explaining such miracles is to recognize that our concept of the "laws" of nature may be too limited, and that other causes, unknown but still within the realm of our experience may be at work.

Some object that such an approach to miracles invites skepticism about the resurrection of Jesus. But this is a special case, very different from the raising of Lazarus; the latter is the resuscitation of a corpse, the return to life of someone who ultimately must die again. The resurrection of Jesus is more properly understood as an eschatological event, something that takes place on the other side of death and history. Even though it happened to a real historical person and has left its traces in history, it cannot be historically verified. All we have is the testimony of those to whom Jesus revealed himself, the "witnesses," and Christianity itself.

If much christological work has deepened our appreciation of the Jesus of history, the work of some theologians has been far more radical. Some are engaged in a speculative reconstruction which pays little attention to the faith of the Church. Thus Jane Schaberg argues that Jesus was illegitimate; for Marianne Sawicki, his birth came about as a result of the rape of his mother.[21] Others have reinterpreted the historical and religious nature

20. Cf. Walter Kasper, *Jesus the Christ* (New York: Paulist, 1977) 90.
21. Jane Schaberg, *The Illegitimacy of Jesus: A Feminist Interpretation of the Infancy Narratives* (San Francisco: Harper & Row, 1987); Marianne Sawicki, *Seeing the*

of his mission. Some theologians, committed to interreligious dialogue, argue that Christian theology should move to an acceptance of genuine pluralism by renouncing its doctrine that salvation is through Christ alone.[22]

Feminist scholarship's particular concern has been the hierarchical and patriarchal structures inherited from Christian history and justified on the basis of the texts of the New Testament. It has been particularly successful in reinterpreting those texts, to present a new picture of the period of Christian origins, particularly through the work of Elisabeth Schüssler Fiorenza. In her ground-breaking book *In Memory of Her,* Schüssler Fiorenza portrays primitive Christianity as an egalitarian movement, like the original "Jesus movement" which she describes as a "discipleship of equals. . . . an inner-Jewish renewal movement that presented an *alternative* option to the dominant patriarchal structures."[23]

Critiquing the gospel tradition to get behind its patriarchal transformation of the authentic Jesus material, she presents a Jesus who saw God not as Abba, despite multiple attestations of this in the tradition, but as Divine Sophia, a female Wisdom figure *(Gestalt),* and himself as Sophia's prophet. Her later book on christology, *Jesus: Miriam's Child, Sophia's Prophet,* makes her methodology even more explicit. She criticizes even Rosemary Ruether for a "heavy reliance on the historical Jesus" which to her is "troublesome" because it remains bound to an understanding of Jesus in masculine terms.[24] Nor will she allow an approach focused on "the option of the historical Jesus for the poor and outcast," for she argues that "we must ground feminist theology on wo/men's struggles for the transformation of kyriarchy" (her term for the rule of some men over others).[25] She is not particularly interested in the historical Jesus; her concern is to "reconfigure the Christian Testament discourses about Jesus not as 'scientific' but as rhetorical."[26]

The Jesus that emerges from her reconstruction proclaims a kingdom without domination or hierarchy, unlike that of the Roman Empire. For this political offense, rather than for religious reasons, he was put to

---

Lord: Resurrection and Early Christian Practice (Minneapolis: Fortress, 1994) 113–15.

22. See *The Myth of Christian Uniqueness: Toward a Pluralistic Theology of Religion,* ed. John Hick and Paul F. Knitter (Maryknoll, N.Y.: Orbis, 1987).

23. Elisabeth Schüssler Fiorenza, *In Memory of Her: A Feminist Reconstruction of Christian Origins* (New York: Crossroad, 1983) 107.

24. Elisabeth Schüssler Fiorenza, *Jesus: Miriam's Child, Sophia's Prophet* (New York: Continuum, 1994) 46–47.

25. Ibid., 48.

26. Ibid., 96.

death. The later tradition "clothed" his story in religious and symbolic language. She rejects the early Christian interpretations of Christ's death as a sacrifice for our sins (cf. 1 Cor 15:3) as "rhetorical accounts."[27] What is at issue in the traditional theology of the cross is the maleness of Jesus, the issue of redemption by a male savior.[28] It is not Jesus' maleness, his manhood which is important, but his liberating practice. But what this approach does is separate the person of Jesus from his work, so that the person ultimately becomes unimportant.

Even more radical is the christology of the Jesus Seminar. Founded by Robert Funk in 1985, the Jesus Seminar claims to be an effort to find the "real" Jesus concealed behind the Gospels and dogma of the Church. In a number of newspaper interviews Funk has singled out conservative Christians and television evangelists, accusing them of keeping the faithful ignorant by continuing to preach a mythical Jesus.[29] But it is the Christ of Christian faith that the Seminar really objects to; its real interest is to replace this Jesus with a secular, non-eschatological Jesus. In 1994 Funk told the *Los Angeles Times* that the Seminar wanted to "liberate" Jesus: "The only Jesus most people want is a mythic one. They don't want the real Jesus. They want the one they can worship. The cultic Jesus."[30] In place of this, the Jesus Seminar offers an alternative gospel, based on their provocative and highly problematic christological reconstruction.

Rejecting the narrative of Mark's Gospel as driven by theological interests, the Seminar's self-selected members try to isolate the earliest strands of the tradition and then vote, using color-coded beads, in order to decide on the authentic words and sayings of Jesus.[31] They reject 82 percent of the sayings of Jesus as inauthentic, including all those that refer to judgment, rewards, and punishments beyond death. What emerges from the remaining disconnected, discrete sayings is a non-eschatological Jesus who bears little resemblance to the one Christians are familiar with, a Jewish sage, wisdom teacher, or Cynic philosopher who enunciates a countercultural critique and is killed, "accidentally crucified," according to Funk.[32]

27. Ibid., 108.

28. Ibid., 97.

29. Luke Timothy Johnson assembles many of these statements in his *The Real Jesus: The Misguided Quest for the Historical Jesus and the Truth of the Traditional Gospels* (San Francisco: HarperSanFrancisco, 1996) 6–20.

30. *Los Angeles Times* (24 February 1994) View Section; cited by Johnson, 7.

31. Cf. *The Five Gospels: The Search for the Authentic Words of Jesus,* new translation and commentary by Robert W. Funk, Roy W. Hoover and the Jesus Seminar (New York: Macmillan, 1993).

32. *Washington Post* (12 November 1988); cited by Johnson, 12.

Marcus Borg seem the most sympathetic to the religious dimensions of Jesus' life. He presents Jesus as a charismatic sage and healer, a spirit person, social prophet, wisdom teacher, and movement founder.[33] As a spirit person, Jesus, like Moses, Ezekiel, Paul, and the Sioux medicine man Black Elk, was "one of many mediators of the sacred."[34] Because Borg seems to identify all eschatology with apocalyptic, he eliminates any talk of the eschatological future from Jesus' preaching. As a social prophet, Jesus challenged the prevailing "politics of purity" of the ruling elites with a "politics of compassion" and so was put to death because of his threatening social vision.

Borg does not deal at length with the resurrection. He grants that the conviction that "God raised Jesus from the dead" is widespread in the New Testament. But he remains by his own admission something of an "agnostic" about an afterlife. He finds the testimony of "near death experiences" as calling into question the adequacy of a materialistic world view. But he is reluctant to move beyond the very general affirmation that there is something beyond death.[35]

John Dominic Crossan is co-chair of the Seminar and one of its most prolific members. Crossan bases much of his reconstruction on non-canonical texts such as the gnostic Gospel of Thomas, the Gospel of Peter, and the secret Gospel of Mark, apocryphal works he considers of value equal to or greater than the canonical Gospels.[36] He presents Jesus as a Jewish Cynic philosopher and "magician" whose sayings advocate a radical egalitarianism, a "kingdom of nuisances and nobodies" that challenged established structures and hierarchical power. He claims "early Christianity knew nothing about the passion of Jesus beyond the fact itself."[37] The first passion narrative, which he claims is the source for Mark's, is attributed to the hypothetical "Cross Gospel," an early version of the

33. Marcus J. Borg, *Jesus, A New Vision: Spirit, Culture, and the Life of Discipleship* (San Francisco: Harper & Row, 1987); *Meeting Jesus Again for the First Time: The Historical Jesus and the Heart of Contemporary Faith* (HarperSanFrancisco, 1994); *Jesus in Contemporary Scholarship* (Valley Forge, Pa.: Trinity Press International, 1994).

34. Borg, *Meeting Jesus Again,* 37.

35. Marcus J. Borg, *The God We Never Knew* (San Francisco: HarperSanFrancisco, 1997) 171–72.

36. John Dominic Crossan, *The Historical Jesus: The Life of a Mediterranean Jewish Peasant* (San Francisco: HarperSanFrancisco, 1991); *Jesus: A Revolutionary Biography* (San Francisco: HarperSanFrancisco, 1994); *The Essential Jesus* (San Francisco: HarperSanFrancisco, 1994).

37. Crossan, *The Historical Jesus,* 387.

apocryphal Gospel of Peter. It represents for Crossan an "historicization" of early passion and parousia prophecies;[38] thus Jesus' passion should be understood as "prophecy historicized" rather than "history remembered." In other words, the passion account was created by an earlier Christian writer on the basis of Old Testament models.

Crossan reduces the resurrection stories to legitimations of the authority of leadership groups in the primitive church, but fails to deal at all with the much earlier Easter kerygma. It is interesting to note that his massive fifteen-page text index in *The Historical Jesus* lists only seven references to Paul's letters, the earliest extent New Testament texts. Few scholars take the Jesus Seminar seriously,[39] though their books remain popular and are often used in undergraduate courses.

Women in the Church

The question of women in the Church is perhaps the most polarizing issue that the Church faces today. Indeed it is one that draws together a number of questions, including inclusive language, theological anthropology, sexuality, the doctrine of God, and the ordination of women. In spite of the controversy these questions have occasioned, the insights emerging from feminist theology have shown the need for rethinking much of what passes for the tradition in regard to women.

The Scriptures themselves, like all expressions of revelation, are historically conditioned, limited both by the knowledge at the time they were written and by the socio-cultural world out of which they came. The biblical culture was patriarchal. The Scriptures were written by men, and were copied, translated, interpreted, and preached by men. It should not be surprising that they tend to reflect the interests of men more than women, or that women's stories have sometimes been suppressed, or their names changed into men's names, or that the texts have been used to justify the subordination of women. Thus Rosemary Ruether argues the need to create a new canon, more inclusive than the biblical one. She suggests including texts taken from the goddess religions, Jewish and Christian apocrypha, as well as Gnostic and feminist sources.[40]

Medieval thinkers contributed to a theology which viewed women as *by nature* inferior, arguing from an ignorance of biology or on the basis of

38. Ibid., 385.

39. Cf. Johnson, *The Real Jesus;* also Raymond E. Brown, *An Introduction to the New Testament* (New York: Doubleday, 1996) 821–22; Richard B. Hayes, "The Corrected Jesus," *First Things* 43 (May 1994) 43–48.

40. Rosemary Radford Ruether, *Womanguides: Readings Toward a Feminist Theology* (Boston, Beacon Press, 1985) ix–xii.

the culturally conditioned understandings of the relation of the sexes. Aquinas gave two arguments for the natural subjection of women to men. First, an individual woman results biologically from some defect in the process of generation, either of the material or from external influences. Second, since reason "predominates" in men, and woman's nature is determined by her reproductive function, woman's "physical" nature is subject to the more spiritual nature of men.[41]

In more recent history the Church has developed a theology of complementarity. In his encyclical on the dignity of women, *Mulieris dignitatem,* Pope John Paul II argues that men and women, created in the image and likeness of God, are equal in dignity, but with a difference. Masculinity and femininity "are distinct, yet at the same time they complete and explain each other." He sees this view in the Letter to the Ephesians, which shows that in the Church "every human being—male and female—is the 'bride,' in that he or she accepts the gift of the love of Christ" (no. 25). Yet only a man, the Pope argues, can take the role of Christ, the bridegroom, towards the Church, the bride of Christ (no. 26).[42] In a "Letter to Women," written shortly before the 1995 Fourth World Conference on Women in Beijing, Pope John Paul returned to the theme of complementarity. "Men and women are complementary. Womanhood expresses the 'human' just as much as manhood does, but in a different and complementary way" (no 7).[43]

Many women today consider such a theology of complementarity seriously flawed. They argue that the theological arguments advanced against the ordination of women are not convincing. Others argue that ordaining women would only perpetuate a hierarchical power structure contrary to the gospel. At the 1995 meeting of the Women's Ordination Conference, held in Arlington, Virginia, a group of the conference planners led by Elisabeth Schüssler Fiorenza urged that the organization work towards a Church without priesthood or hierarchy.[44] They called for new expressions of ministry and Eucharist, as we will see below.

41. Aquinas, *Summa Theologiae* I, 92, 1: see Marie Anne Mayeski, "Excluded by the Logic of Control: Women in Medieval Society and Scholastic Theology," in *Equal at the Creation: Sexism, Society, and Christian Thought,* ed. Joseph Martos and Pierre Hegy (Toronto: University of Toronto Press, 1998) 87–89.

42. John Paul II, *Mulieris dignitatem; Origins* 18/17 (1988) 278–79.

43. John Paul II, "Letter to Women," *Origins* 25/9 (1995) 141.

44. See Peter Steinfels, "Women Wary About Aiming to Be Priests," *New York Times,* November 14, 1995.

Authority

According to Catholic theology, the Church has had a principle of order, and thus, a primitive "hierarchy," from the beginning.[45] During his ministry Jesus called "the Twelve" from the larger group of his disciples. Symbolically, they represented the twelve tribes of Israel, and thus the whole community of the disciples as a renewed Israel. But the Twelve also exercised real authority in the primitive community. Though the New Testament recognizes a wider group of apostles who like the Twelve were witnesses to the resurrection, the latter, who had known Jesus during his historical ministry and had been personally chosen by him, functioned as a kind of apostolic council, guiding the primitive community in decisions that affected its life. The origins of the Church's ordained ministry is a complex process; it cannot be reduced to the apostles appointing bishops who in turn ordained others. Still, there is historical evidence for the apostles sharing their ministry with others, from which emerged an official ministry which was seen by the biblical authors as well as by the later tradition as linked to their authority.

There is much that could be done to change the way that authority is exercised in the Church today. For example, the monarchical style of papal authority, the product of the Middle Ages which reached its apogee in the period after Vatican I, is only one way of exercising primacy; it is not faithful to the great tradition of the first millennium. Pope John Paul II himself has invited theologians and Church leaders from different traditions to help him "find a way of exercising the primacy which, while in no way renouncing what is essential to its mission, is nonetheless open to a new situation."[46] In other words, the present, highly centralized style of papal ministry, with all decisions stemming from Rome, is not the only possible one.

It would not be contrary to the Catholic tradition to give the Synod of Bishops more power, even on occasion to exercise a deliberative rather than a merely consultative vote, a possibility allowed for by canon law (can. 343). Canon law also recognizes the possibility of local churches choosing their own bishops, rather than having them simply appointed by Rome (can. 375). Archbishop John Quinn, in responding to the Pope's invitation, has suggested such reforms; he has also urged that the Roman Curia be reformed, that the bishops be allowed to exercise a "true, active collegiality and not merely a passive collegiality," and that the principle

45. See Terence L. Nichols, *That All May Be One: Hierarchy and Participation in the Church* (Collegeville: The Liturgical Press, 1997).

46. *Ut unum sint,* no. 95; see *Origins* 25 (1995) 69.

of subsidiarity be honored in the government of the Church.[47] All this could be accomplished without challenging the principle of the Church's hierarchical nature.

But feminist scholarship, particularly through the work of Elisabeth Schüssler Fiorenza, has challenged the very principle of order, particularly its hierarchical expression in the tradition. According to her reconstruction, the egalitarian spirit of the original Jesus movement was continued in the early Christian missionary movement and their communities; both men and women in principle had equal access to positions of authority and leadership. But within the later New Testament period there was a shift from equal access and communal authority to a restrictive patriarchal leadership based on the male heads of households, to the obvious disadvantaging of women.[48]

There is much to commend Schüssler Fiorenza's work. It has led to an important recovery of the prominent roles women played within the earliest Christian communities, and she has made scholars much more aware of the fact that our access to primitive Christianity is through texts and traditions selected, transmitted, and interpreted by males. Adapting the perspective of liberation theology which challenges the objectivity of academic theology,[49] she argues that feminist theology, like all liberation theologies, must take an "advocacy stance," refusing to grant oppressive and destructive texts or traditions revelatory authority.[50]

But feminist reconstruction should not assert more than can be clearly established or affirm what is contrary to the historical evidence. One cannot simply ignore the frequent references to the Twelve, the Three, and Peter amidst the disciples in the tradition, or reduce the role of the Twelve to eschatological symbol rather than actual historical leadership. The fact that Paul ultimately sought the approval of those "reputed to be pillars," James, Kephas, and John (Gal 2:9), for the way he carried out his Gentile mission is evidence that he recognized a special authority of those who had belonged to the inner circle of Jesus' disciples.[51]

---

47. See John R. Quinn, "The Exercise of the Primacy: Facing the Cost of Christian Unity," *Commonweal* 133 (12 July 1996) 11–20; also Thomas P. Rausch, "Archbishop Quinn's Challenge: A Not Impossible Task," in *The Exercise of Primacy,* ed. Phyllis Zagano and Terrence W. Tilley (New York: Crossroad, 1998) 47–64.

48. *In Memory of Her,* 286–87.

49. Ibid., 6.

50. Ibid., 33.

51. Bengt Holmberg, *Paul and Power: The Structure of Authority in the Primitive Church as Reflected in the Pauline Epistles* (Philadelphia: Fortress, 1980) 27–28.

An egalitarian interpretation of primitive Christianity such as one finds in some commentators[52] reflects more an anachronistic reading of the data through modern lenses than a critical retrieval; it is not history but ideological reconstruction.

Eucharist and Ministry

The apparent inability of the official Church to come to terms with the question of ordaining women and married men has led to considerable anger and frustration. Avery Dulles accused speakers at the 1997 convention of the prestigious Catholic Theological Society of America of mounting "a series of attacks on Catholic doctrine more radical, it would seem, than the challenges issued by Luther and Calvin." Specifically, he charged them with rejecting fundamental articles of Catholic belief regarding priesthood and Eucharist expressed by the magisterial tradition since Trent.[53]

His critique was in some ways exaggerated, but it was not entirely inaccurate. Peter Steinfels acknowledged that Dulles's argument was not well served by his citations. But he also observed that all three addresses "moved in a similar direction, a direction away from positions taken from Trent through Vatican II and toward positions much more congenial to the Reformers and in general to their liberal and low-church descendants."[54] For example, one speaker pointed to contemporary trends as heralding an exciting new future of eucharistic practice without ordained presiders.[55]

On a pastoral level, a growing number of communities, appealing to this low-church, congregational theology, are celebrating eucharistic services without a priest. There are well over one hundred groups of women in the United States today who gather regularly for their own eucharistic celebrations without ordained presiders. Leadership is shared; in some groups the role of presider is rotated, in others all join in the reading of the Eucharistic Prayer, or share the different parts among those present.[56] Those involved argue that they are returning to the roots of early Christianity,

52. Cf. Edward Schillebeeckx, *The Church With a Human Face* (New York: Crossroad, 1985) 37–39; Sandra M. Schneiders, "Evangelical Equality," *Spirituality Today* 38 (1986) 11.

53. "Disputed Questions: How Catholic is the CTSA? Three Views," Avery Dulles, Mary Ann Donovan, Peter Steinfels, *Commonweal* 125/6 (27 March 1998) 13.

54. Ibid., 16–17.

55. Gary Macy, "The Eucharist and Popular Religiosity," *CTSA Proceedings* 52 (1997) 57–58.

56. See Sheila Durkin Dierks, *WomanEucharist* (Boulder, Colo.: WovenWord Press, 1997).

that the Eucharist predates the hierarchy, that all are priests in virtue of the universal priesthood, that a group of Christians gathered in Christ's name is a sacrament, that they are simply responding to the movement of the Spirit.[57] The celebrant or leader "is deemed to be one who carries out the will of the whole community to ask God's presence. Thus the leader acts on the desire of the celebrants by putting their prayer, their desire for unity with Christ, into action. This more clearly reflects the position of the early Church than the system of separation and elevation long in favor. *This is ancient ecclesiology.*"[58] Or at least, this is the argument, though it is far from certain or capable of demonstration.

While it is true that the whole assembly celebrates the Eucharist, to overemphasize the assembly as the subject of the liturgical action without equal attention to the role of the ordained presider implies that the latter is not really necessary, a conclusion that some are quick to draw. The Eucharist is constitutive of the Church, not just spiritually, but in its embodied, historical reality, including its hierarchical structure (LG 8). To deny the link between office and Eucharist or to overlook the visible bonds of communion which join communities to the Church local and universal is to risk dissolving the Church into a plurality of self-authorizing groups, thus substituting a congregationalism for Catholicism.

Conclusions

Catholic theology has come a long way in the years since the Second Vatican Council. It is no longer a work done almost exclusively by clerics, nor is it bound to the categories and methods of neoscholasticism. It is a critical discipline and finds its home today primarily in the academy.

In Catholic colleges and universities theology in a very real sense serves as the integrating discipline within the curriculum, for it involves the literary analysis of texts, philosophical and historical criticism, socio-political and cultural studies, and the disciplined integration of reason with faith. In a preeminent sense theology is at the service of the mission of a Catholic university, as that mission is rooted in a theological wisdom, specifically, in the Christian vision of the reconciliation of all people to God in Jesus.

Yet the loosening of the bonds between theology and Church authority has been a mixed blessing. While new theologies and theological methods have enriched the Church's understanding of the mystery of God's presence in Christ, the critical dimension of theology has often overshad-

57. Ibid., 82–83, 106–108, 122–23.
58. Ibid., 158.

owed its role as a work of the Church. The result has been a tension between theology and Church. At the same time, the recent efforts of the Roman authorities to discipline dissenting theologians, to require all of them to seek a mandatum, and to extend the authority of the magisterium have heightened this tension.

Theology must always be a reflection on faith. The Christian community, the Church, with its promise of the assistance of the Spirit, remains the primary bearer and transmitter of the faith.[59] The theologian needs to be rooted in that faith community, in its life, its worship, the struggle of its members to live as disciples. This is always primary, for theology represents a language of reflection several levels removed from the encounter with the mystery of God in faith mediated by the biblical word, the liturgy, and the sacraments of the Church. When it becomes cut off from the Church's worship and life, it loses its proper theological character and runs the risk of becoming simply another ideology.

59. Cf. Avery Dulles, *The Craft of Theology,* 8–9.

3

The New Apologists

How can the Catholic Church best carry out its mission in the contemporary world? As the twentieth century draws to a close, two different but related approaches to this question are increasingly put forward. One stresses the need for apologetics, presenting the claims of Catholic Christianity to nonbelievers and defending the Catholic Church against the arguments of other Christian communities, particularly those fundamentalist and evangelical Christians who are now targeting Catholics in their own proselytizing efforts. In recent years a whole new group of Catholic apologists has appeared, with writers and speakers such as Karl Keating, Peter Kreeft, Thomas Howard, the late Sheldon Vanauken, Scott Hahn, Patrick Madrid, and Mark Shea prominent among them.

The other approach stresses the need for a new evangelization, one that will carry the good news of salvation in Christ to those who have never heard it as well as to those in cultures and countries formerly Christian who no longer practice their faith. Vatican II placed a new emphasis on evangelization as central to the mission of the Church and during the pontificates of Paul VI and John Paul II it has assumed an even greater importance.[1]

Apologetics has been an important part of Christian theology since its beginning, though in more recent times the term itself has fallen into disuse except in more conservative circles. Conversely, evangelization is a relatively new term for Catholics; it came into Catholic literature in the middle of the present century, partly through the influence of Karl Barth

---

1. See Avery Dulles, "John Paul and the New Evangelization," *America* 166 (1992) 53–57.

and partly because of the important place it occupies in the documents of Vatican II.

In this chapter I would like to, first, look briefly at the history of apologetics, second, consider its latest manifestation in what I will call the "new apologists," and finally, raise the question, "Why are so many Catholics today joining other churches?"

Apologetics

The Greek word *apologia* means a speech in defense of some idea or philosophy or way of life. Some of the earliest post-New Testament Christian theological works were apologies written to defend Christian faith and practices against both Jewish and pagan critics. A list would include Justin Martyr's *First* and *Second Apology* and his *Dialogue with Trypho the Jew,* Aristides' *Apology,* and Athenagoras' *Supplication for Christians* and *On the Resurrection of the Dead* in the second century; Clement of Alexandria's *Protrepticus,* Origen's *Contra Celsum,* Tertullian's *To the Pagans* and *Apology,* Arnobius' *Case Against the Pagans* in the third century; and Eusebius' *Preparation of the Gospel* and *Proof of the Gospel* in the fourth. These early Christian apologists entered into dialogue with Greco-Roman theology, criticizing its mythical and civil expressions but often showing appreciation for its philosophical insights.

Medieval theology continued the apologetic tradition, though now it was focused against Islam and Judaism. Abelard developed a rational defense of Christianity in his *Dialogue Between a Philosopher, a Jew and a Christian*. Thomas Aquinas's *Summa Contra Gentiles* was directed against a diversity of challenges from Greek and Arab scholars; some manuscripts carry the title *On the Truth of the Catholic Faith Against Unbelievers.*

The fierce controversies between Christians that resulted from the Reformation turned apologetics into controversial theology. Faith and works, Scripture and tradition, and controverted questions in ecclesiology were now the focus of polemical apologists on both sides. At the same time, in the centuries following the Reformation apologetics became much more comprehensive, broadening its scope from controversial issues to a concern for the scientific and methodological foundations of the faith.

The career of John Henry Newman (1801–1890), perhaps one of the greatest apologists of all time, spanned the nineteenth century. Johann Sebastian von Drey (1777–1853), the founder of the Tübingen School, developed the idea that apologetics was an independent discipline, prior to theology, which would demonstrate and defend Christianity's foundation in revelation. Johann Nepomuk Ehrlich, a professor at the University of

Prague, took Drey's work further, articulating a new theological discipline he called "fundamental theology."[2] Fundamental theology combines in one discipline both the defense of the faith and the attempt to establish its rational foundations.

Twentieth-Century Apologetics

By the beginning of the twentieth century two basic types of apologetics had emerged, "a defensive type that seeks to argue unbelievers into submission to the faith as traditionally understood and a revisionist type that seeks to forge a new synthesis between religious and secular knowledge."[3] The latter type, exemplified by theologians such as Maurice Blondel, Pierre Rousselot, Léonce de Grandmaison, and Jean Guitton, represented the best in the tradition of Catholic theology. These scholars tried to reach beyond the narrow confines of scholastic theology to express Christian faith in terms more intelligible to modern ways of thinking. Not all of their efforts were successful. The Modernists went too far in seeking a reconciliation with modernity, and were repudiated by the Church.

As the Church reacted to what it perceived as the threat of modernism it encouraged a more defensive apologetics. The Roman manuals used in seminaries generally followed a two-part organization; first, an argument based on miracles and prophecies to "prove" the truth of Christianity and the divine authority of Christ, then a demonstration that the Church founded by Christ is the same as the present Catholic Church. This was rhetorically effective for arguing Catholic claims, but not really credible in terms of proper theological method.

Prior to the Second Vatican Council, students in Catholic colleges and universities were formed in this kind of defensive apologetics. They did not study theology; instead they took courses in "religion," designed to hand on the faith and often taught by instructors who lacked the credentials required by other departments.[4] Usually the curriculum included a course called simply "apologetics." Students read authors such as Arnold Lunn, Karl Adam, Ronald Knox, Robert Hugh Benson, Frank Sheed, C. S. Lewis (an Anglican), Hilaire Belloc, Christopher Dawson, and of course, Gilbert Keith Chesterton. Who from that time can forget struggling with the dense prose and paradoxes in Chesterton's *The Everlasting Man?* A good number of these apologists were converts to Catholicism, among

2. See Francis Schüssler Fiorenza, *Foundational Theology: Jesus and the Church* (New York: Crossroad, 1984) 261.

3. Avery Dulles, *A History of Apologetics* (New York: Corpus, 1971) 202.

4. Robert J. Wister, "The Teaching of Theology 1950–90: the American Catholic Experience," *America* 162 (1990) 92.

them Knox, Benson, Lunn, and Chesterton. If their works were popular, they were generally in tune with the dominant theology of the times; that is, they reflected the authoritarian and rationalist theology of the Roman manuals and were almost completely untouched by newer currents such as the biblical and liturgical renewals.

This defensive apologetics did not represent the best aspects of the apologetic tradition. The early apologists defended Christianity from its critics by appealing to the superiority of the Christian understanding of God and the moral quality of Christian life, sometimes drawing on Greek and Roman philosophy in the process. Some, like Justin Martyr and Clement of Alexandria, attempted to show how the best insights of pagan philosophy were more fully illumined by Christian revelation. In the fourth and fifth centuries apologists used Platonic and Neoplatonic thought to express their theology. In the process they developed a theological literature that treated the great themes of the faith. The scholastic theologians explored the relations between faith and reason. Aquinas took on the Averroists by Christianizing Aristotle; for this some of his teachings were condemned shortly after his death at both Paris and Oxford. Blondel's "method of immanence" sought to find a place for the supernatural within the scientific worldview of his day. In the twentieth century Karl Adam drew on the phenomenology of Scheler, Rahner was influenced by his study of Heidegger, von Balthasar used the personalism of Martin Buber, and Teilhard de Chardin sought to interpret Christianity within an evolutionary framework.

Not all Christian apologists were as able to draw on contemporary culture and science for their work. They were not above using their rhetorical skills to their own advantage, and their work often reflects the limitations of a precritical age. Some sounded hostile to the role of reason in the understanding of the faith. Tertullian's outburst is famous: "What has Jerusalem to do with Athens, the Church with the Academy, the Christian with the heretic. . . . I have no use for a Stoic or a Platonic or a dialectic Christianity. After Jesus Christ we have no need of speculation, after the Gospel no need of research."[5] Others were hostile towards their opponents. Chrysostom's eight *Homilies against the Jews* contain some classic examples of Christian anti-Semitism. Pascal was suspicious of critical reason even while he used it to analyze the psychological and intuitive side of human consciousness; his emphasis on "reasons of the heart" called attention to the important place of subjectivity in religious experience.

---

5. Tertullian, "Prescription Against the Heretics," LCC 5, 36; *Early Latin Theology,* trans. and ed. S. L. Greenslade (Philadelphia: Westminster Press, 1956) 36.

But those who were able to enter into dialogue with their culture represented the best of Christian apologetics; they saw the philosophical or scientific modes of discourse of their time, not as inimical to the faith, but as resources to be used in its defense and expression. In doing so they contributed immeasurably to the development of theology as a science.

Vatican II marked the end of the old, defensive apologetics. In contemporary theology, apologetics is usually seen as a part of fundamental theology, sometimes called "foundational" theology. An outstanding example of fundamental theology with a strong apologetic interest would be Karl Rahner's *Foundations of Christian Faith*. Other contemporary examples might include Hans Küng's *On Being a Christian*, Joseph Ratzinger's *Introduction to Christianity*, and Gerald O'Collins's *Fundamental Theology*.

The New Apologists

However the last decade or so has seen the emergence of a new Catholic apologetics, much of it of the defensive type. In part it represents a protest to what is perceived as a secularized liberal theology as well as a reaction to modernity in general. And in part it represents a response to those fundamentalist and evangelical communities which have been so successful at attracting Catholics into their congregations. But whatever their primary motivation, these new apologists are deeply suspicious of modern theological scholarship.

Who are these new apologists? As a group they are highly diverse. Some are faculty members at established Catholic institutions of higher education, for example, Peter Kreeft and Ronald Tacelli, S.J., at Boston College, Thomas Howard at St. John's Seminary, Brighton, Massachusetts, and Mitch Pacwa, S.J., a frequent guest on Mother Angelica's EWTN. Others are at conservative Catholic colleges like Steubenville or Christendom College, and still others like Karl Keating, Patrick Madrid, Mark Shea, David Currie, Gerry Matatics, Steve and Karen Wood, and Keith Fournier are involved with a host of conservative organizations, mail order ministries, and publishing houses.[6]

One of the most popular is Karl Keating, the director of a lay organization called *Catholic Answers* which publishes a monthly journal of apologetics, *This Rock*. Many of them, as in the early part of the century, are converts, among them Dale Vree, Peter Kreeft, Scott and Kimberly Hahn, Thomas Howard, and Sheldon Vanauken (d. 1996), all of them associated

---

6. Cf. Peter A. Huff, "New Apologists in America's Conservative Catholic Subculture," *Horizons* 23/2 (1996) 242–60.

with *The New Oxford Review*. In speaking of their conversions, they express a common concern for the state of contemporary Christianity, pointing in particular to the ordination of women, the increasing acceptance of homosexuality and abortion, and the lack of an authoritative magisterium in their former Protestant churches.[7] They are part of a spectrum of conservative Catholicism as we saw earlier.

Keating's *Catholicism and Fundamentalism* is a best-seller.[8] The first part presents a useful documented history of fundamentalist anti-Catholicism. The second part, in which he takes on specific fundamentalist charges against Catholicism, shows him not as an angry critic, but as one who generally speaks with respect for his opponents. But the third part—which shifts from a criticism of fundamentalism to one of Protestantism in general—also reveals his lack of sympathy for mainstream Roman Catholic theology. While his recommended sources include some classic references such as Joseph Tixeront's *History of Dogmas,* Johannes Quasten's *Patrology,* Ludwig Ott's *Fundamentals of Catholic Dogma,* and John Henry Newman's *Essay on the Development of Christian Doctrine,* many of them are pre-Vatican II works untouched by the theological renewal that preceded the council. Thus he prefers the 1914 *Catholic Encyclopedia* to the 1967 *New Catholic Encyclopedia* ("inferior in coverage but adequate"),[9] and recommends the 1953 *A Catholic Commentary on Holy Scripture* which uses the Douay-Rheims translation. He mentions *A New Catholic Commentary on Holy Scripture* (1969) and, more cautiously, *The Jerome Biblical Commentary* (advising that "the orthodox Catholic can skip the more tendentious essays"),[10] and seems to prefer William G. Most's *Free from All Error*. William Most was an ultra-conservative Catholic apologist who labored to defend positions such as the historicity of the infancy narratives or the idea that Vatican II did not reverse previous magisterial teachings.[11]

Scott Hahn came to Catholicism from a background in evangelical Presbyterianism, followed four years later by his wife Kimberly. He received his master of divinity degree from Gordon-Conwell Theological Seminary and served as a pastor for a number of years prior to his con-

7. Dan O'Neill, *The New Catholics: Contemporary Converts Tell Their Stories* (New York: Crossroad, 1987).

8. Karl Keating, *Catholicism and Fundamentalism: The Attack on "Romanism" by "Bible Christians"* (San Francisco: Ignatius, 1988).

9. Ibid., 321.

10. Ibid., 324.

11. See William G. Most, *Catholic Apologetics Today: Answers to Modern Critics* (Rockford, Ill.: Tan Books, 1986).

version; afterwards he did doctoral work in systematic theology at Marquette, receiving his degree in 1995. He presently teaches at Franciscan University of Steubenville.

The compelling story of his conversion, first taped in 1989, has led to over two hundred audio and video cassettes, released through Saint Joseph Communications, circulating now in many countries, as well as a book. It tells of his turning to the Catholic Church as he was reluctantly forced to admit that the two pillars of the Reformation, first *sola fide* and then the *sola scriptura* principle, collapsed in the light his study of Scripture.[12]

Hahn is particularly effective in discussions with evangelical Protestants since his theological approach is similar to theirs, responding to each question with an appropriate biblical text, even offering a biblical explanation of indulgences or for the Catholic position on birth control. But he has also done an impressive doctoral dissertation on the biblical theology of covenants. He is one of a growing number of Protestant pastors from evangelical backgrounds, many from Gordon-Conwell, who have been received into the Catholic Church.[13] One of them, Marcus Grodi, directs a support group for Protestant clergy and their families moving towards the Catholic Church called the *Coming Home Network International,* based at Steubenville. Its goal "is to help reverse the deleterious effects of the Reformation."[14] As of January 1999, the CHNetwork claimed some six thousand members.

If some of the new apologists are concerned primarily with proving the truth claims of the Catholic Church against Protestant criticism, those associated with the *New Oxford Review* have a broader, more sophisticated focus. They combine a theological conservatism with an evangelical critique of contemporary culture, based on the biblical text, the natural law tradition, and the authority of the magisterium. They mourn the loss of a world of meaning which they see as having given purpose to human life, and they are willing to wrestle with basic issues of truth, revelation, grace, the problem of evil, life, death, and God. They write not as systematicians, exegetes, or biblical theologians but as deeply engaged believers; their backgrounds are in philosophy, political theory, and literature, not

12. See Scott and Kimberly Hahn, *Rome Sweet Home: Our Journey to Catholicism* (San Francisco: Ignatius, 1993).

13. See Elizabeth Altham, "Protestant Pastors on the Road to Rome," *Sursum Corda!* Special Promotional Edition, no date [1996] 2–13; see also Kenneth H. Howell, "The New Surge of Converts to Rome from Protestantism," *New Oxford Review* 63 (March 1996) 21–23.

14. *The Coming Home Newsletter* (June–August 1996) 2.

theology. Looking to Chesterton and C. S. Lewis as models, they share their experience in the effort to reach into ours with their words. In their uncompromising defense of the Catholic tradition as articulated by the magisterium on controversial questions such as sexuality, celibacy, and the rights of women in Church and society, they offer a strong alternative to a secular culture. Most importantly, they are attempting to articulate for modern men and women an evangelical vision of Christian faith that is Catholic rather than Protestant.

There is something both admirable and appealing about these converts, their desire to be part of one universal Church, their frustration with the variety of biblical interpretations in Protestantism, often dependent on a charismatic local pastor or group of independent Bible churches, their appreciation of the authority and doctrinal clarity coming from Rome, their astonishment at the Catholic character of the ancient Christian tradition, the wonderful discovery of Christ's real presence in the Eucharist. Some, like Scott Hahn, have a gift for presenting the Christian mysteries in a fresh and appealing way.

But their encounter with the contemporary Catholic Church in its local incarnations is often unsettling for them. They are too ready to see "false teaching" and "disobedience" in contemporary theology or catechetics or to identify orthodox Catholicism with its most conservative expressions, for example, the Franciscan University of Steubenville or Mother Angelica's Eternal Word Television Network. They are relentlessly hostile to contemporary Catholic theology precisely because it is critical. They object to what they see as contemporary theology's relativistic and subjective approach to religious questions, its substitution of "values clarification" for "objective truth" and "objective values" in the area of morals, particularly sexual morals.[15] Those doing contemporary theology are dismissed as "neomodernists," while their own approach is consciously premodern. Kreeft and Tacelli specifically call for a return to a medieval understanding of reason.[16]

A Precritical Theology

The antimodern, precritical approach of many of the new apologists shows them to represent a Catholic type of fundamentalism, or as it is often called by Catholic scholars, integralism. According to John Quinn, former archbishop of San Francisco,

15. Ibid., 16–19.
16. Peter Kreeft and Ronald K. Tacelli, *Handbook of Christian Apologetics* (Downers Grove, Ill.: InterVarsity, 1994) 14–15.

Integralism is not true orthodoxy. True orthodoxy knows that the church grows in its understanding and in its expression of the faith. True orthodoxy knows that not everything is a matter of faith. Integralism admits no changes and, worse, no growth. It stifles the Spirit, deifies the past, and lives, not in hope, but in perpetual fear.[17]

Too often the new apologists' use of Scripture is biblicist rather than critical or hermeneutical. They ignore the Bible's complex historical development, use it to proof-text doctrinal and moral concerns, and interpret gospel sayings attributed to Jesus historically rather than distinguishing the various levels of the gospel tradition. Karl Keating argues that all the New Testament books were written prior to the fall of Jerusalem in the year 70.[18]

At the same time many of them exhibit a fundamentalist understanding of teaching, one that fails to note the historical context of a doctrinal statement, its degree of authority, and the possibility of doctrinal development or even change. Their textual interpretation, whether biblical or magisterial, and their approach to the development of authority, structure, and doctrine shows signs of the same non-historical consciousness that one associates with Protestant fundamentalism.

From an ecumenical perspective, the new apologists raise the dilemma of a divided Christianity, with its innumerable competing churches chosen on the basis of personal preference—some twenty-eight thousand according to Scott Hahn—in a powerful way. They have helped a considerable number of Protestant pastors find a new home in the Catholic Church and brought many Catholics back to the Church. But as Peter Huff observes, "many of the new apologists share the anti-Protestant instincts of the preconciliar Catholic revival writers,"[19] apologists such as G. K. Chesterton, Ronald Knox, and Hilaire Belloc. Their approach to other Christian communities is more often polemical than irenic. Rather than seeking to find areas of agreement, as does official Catholic ecumenism, they tend to reject mainline Protestantism, not just for its contemporary pluralism and embrace of modernity, but also in some of its foundational doctrines.

Their philosophical outlook, particularly for those who come from evangelical backgrounds, reflects what George Marsden identifies as

17. John R. Quinn, "Response," in *The Exercise of the Primacy,* ed. Phyllis Zagano and Terrence W. Tilley (New York: Crossroad, 1998) 110.
18. See his *No Apology from the New Apologists* (San Diego: Catholic Answers, 1997) 13–18.
19. Huff, "New Apologists," 251.

"Scottish Common Sense Realism."[20] They continue to adhere to an exaggerated natural/supernatural dualism and a supernatural rationalism which tends to see the Bible rather than Jesus as God's supreme revelation. In this way they seek to secure the tradition from the changes brought on by the "acids of modernity." But this identification of God's revelation with the text is itself a postmodern solution.

If truth is to be found primarily in the text rather than in the Christ-event, modern criticism is not really necessary; the meaning of the biblical text is self-evident to those who approached it with ordinary common sense.[21] The result is an overly confident dogmatism, one that gives simple answers to complex questions. Engaging fundamentalists on their own terms rather than by means of critical biblical and historical scholarship gives their arguments a certain strength. But their arguments are based on an often simplistic interpretation of biblical and patristic texts. This suggests a fundamentalism of their own, though one that adds the magisterial document to the biblical text. Some examples.

Keating's *Catholicism and Fundamentalism* exemplifies this precritical, common sense approach. He seems uninterested in the methods the Catholic Church uses today in doing biblical interpretation. Moving quickly from the Bible, "considered merely as a history," to the truth of Jesus' claim to divinity, he reasons Jesus could not have been . . . merely a good man who was not God "because no merely good man would make the claims he made." But this effort to establish the divinity of Jesus simply on the basis of statements attributed to him by the evangelists confuses historical and theological levels of the text. Next he moves to Jesus' promise to establish a Church, from there to the Church's necessary infallibility to accomplish what Jesus said it must, and finally to the Church's infallible teaching of the Bible's inspired character.[22]

Keating routinely takes statements attributed to Jesus by the evangelists as his literal, historical words. For example, in discussing the Eucharist, he takes the Bread of Life discourse in John 6 as the historical words of Jesus rather than as the eucharistic theology of the Johannine community.[23] What the 1993 Biblical Commission document, *The Interpretation*

20. George M. Marsden, *Fundamentalism and American Culture: The Shaping of Twentieth-Century Evangelicalism: 1870–1925* (New York/Oxford: Oxford University Press, 1980) 14–16; see also his *Understanding Fundamentalism and Evangelicalism* (Grand Rapids, Mich.: William B. Eerdmans, 1991) 117–19.

21. See Mark A. Noll, *The Scandal of the Evangelical Mind* (Grand Rapids, Mich.: Eerdmans, 1994) 90–107.

22. Keating, *Catholicism and Fundamentalism,* 125.

23. Ibid., 232.

of the Bible in the Church, says of fundamentalists could also be said of Keating: "In what concerns the Gospels, fundamentalism does not take into account the development of the gospel tradition, but naïvely confuses the final stage of this tradition (what the evangelists have written) with the initial (the words and deeds of the historical Jesus."[24]

His approach to history is similar. He refutes Jimmy Swaggart's argument on the nonexistence of the early papacy simply by referring to the tradition's naming Linus as the second pope.[25] Swaggart may be ignorant of that tradition, but the emergence of the Petrine ministry is far more complex. Rome did not have a monoepiscopal government until close to A.D. 150. Nor should Keating take as historical without further question Tertullian's statement that Clement was ordained by Peter,[26] something that would be questioned by most historians today.

Keating's approach to the Church's teaching authority is particularly unnuanced; it represents a new kind of non-historical orthodoxy. Too easily ascribing infallibility to the ordinary magisterium, he maintains that the doctrine enunciated by *Humanae vitae* is infallibly taught because it represents the unanimous teaching of authority.[27] Most commentators would disagree.[28] He argues repeatedly that no pope has ever contradicted the teaching of an earlier pope and no ecumenical council has ever contradicted the teaching of an earlier council on faith or morals.[29] This suggests that what has once been taught by authority in the area of faith or morals can never change. Yet today, an increasing number of studies on reception illustrate how what has been the consistent teaching of the ordinary magisterium on questions such as the impossibility of salvation outside the Church, the tolerance of slavery, sanctioned by Lateran IV (1215), Florence (1442), and Lateran V (1516), and the justification of the use of torture by Lateran III (1179) and Vienne (1311), has been changed or even reversed because of the way in which it was received by the Church.[30] A presentation of the

24. Pontifical Biblical Commission, *The Interpretation of the Bible in the Church, Origins* 23 (1994) 510.

25. Keating, *Catholicism and Fundamentalism,* 92.

26. Ibid., 202.

27. Ibid., 218.

28. For both sides of this debate, see Joseph A. Komonchak, "*Humanae vitae* and its Reception: Ecclesiological Reflections," 221–57 and John C. Ford and Germain Grisez, "Contraception and Infallibility," 258–312, in *Theological Studies* 39 (1978).

29. Ibid., 219.

30. Cf. Luis M. Bermejo, *Infallibility on Trial: Church, Conciliarity and Communion* (Westminster, Md.: Christian Classics, 1992) 252–64; 309–40; also *Rome Has Spoken: A Guide to Forgotten Papal Statements and How They Have Changed Through the Centuries,* ed. Maureen Fiedler and Linda Rabben (New York: Crossroad, 1998).

Catholic tradition able to acknowledge not just development, but also change in the doctrinal tradition is a more honest one.

One can find a similar biblicist, common sense approach in Peter Kreeft's apologetics, for example, in his approach to christology which fails to distinguish the various levels in the gospel tradition, thus taking as historical Jesus saying "Before Abraham was, I AM,"[31] or in the physicalism he employs to describe Catholic eucharistic faith: "It has . . . not ceased to amaze me, that Almighty God suffers me to touch him, move him and eat him! Imagine! When I move my hand to my mouth with the Host, I move God through space. When I put him here, he is here. When I put him there, he is there."[32] The tradition has been very reluctant to use such literal language as it reduces sacramental presence to material physicality, thus denying the transcendence of God.

Kreeft accuses theologians of "not attacking the errors of the world but attacking the truths of the faith."[33] In his own work he tries to walk a careful path between fundamentalism and modernism—which he identifies with those who "interpret everything, or at least everything miraculous or supernatural (or morally unpopular) nonliterally."[34] Yet his all or nothing approach to miracles sets up a false alternative. Many contemporary mainstream Catholic scholars, for example Bishop Walter Kasper, now secretary of the Pontifical Council for Promoting Christian Unity, or John P. Meier, distinguish between the basically historical tradition of the healing miracles of Jesus and the "nature miracles," which Kasper calls "secondary accretions to the original tradition," many of them being legendary.[35] Bishop Kasper is certainly not a modernist.

J. P. Meier in his exhaustive examination of the miracle tradition in the second volume of his work on christology, *A Marginal Jew,* takes a similar position. He concludes that "the statement that Jesus acted as and was viewed as an exorcist and healer during his public ministry has as much historical corroboration as almost any other statement we can make about the Jesus of history."[36] Though Meier, like many scholars, sees the nature miracles as the creation of the early Church, he argues that the tradition of

31. Peter Kreeft, *Fundamentals of the Faith: Essays in Christian Apologetics* (San Francisco: Ignatius, 1988) 60.

32. Ibid., 282.

33. Ibid., 13.

34. Peter Kreeft and Ronald K. Tacelli, *Handbook of Christian Apologetics,* 205.

35. Walter Kasper, *Jesus the Christ* (New York: Paulist, 1977) 90.

36. John P. Meier, *A Marginal Jew: Rethinking the Historical Jesus,* vol. II (New York: Doubleday, 1994) 970.

Jesus raising the dead goes back to some event in Jesus' ministry, and offers a similar argument for the story of the feeding of the multitude.

Such a nuanced approach to the miracle tradition neither leads to nor requires a denial of the resurrection of Jesus. Mainline Catholic scholars such as these do not reduce the resurrection to a change in the understanding of the disciples; it was something that really happened to Jesus, a real event which has left its imprint on history even if its eschatological nature means that it cannot be "proved." However they are careful to avoid the unnuanced language and often literalist approach of more conservative commentators.

Meeting a Genuine Need

The work of the new apologists appeals to many Catholics today. Many of them are poorly instructed in their faith. With little knowledge of history or of their own tradition, they find their own faith strengthened by an approach which gives clear answers with such apparent authority. Others, concerned or even frightened by the direction of contemporary Catholic theology, welcome what they consider an "orthodox" presentation of their faith, even if it means a return to a more defensive Catholicism. Many will say that the new apologists have brought them back to the Church. This includes a considerable number of seminarians and young religious.

A number of commentators have remarked on the conservative orientation of those entering seminaries and religious life today. Robert Schreiter cautions that those directing their formation programs need to be aware of their own bias when they describe younger candidates for the religious life as "conservative." He points out that these formators came of age during the 1960s and early 1970s, influenced by the council and the cultural upheaval of the late 1960s. But for today's candidates, "all that they have experienced religiously and in other dimensions of their lives has been discontinuity and fragmentation." Their "conservatism" may actually represent a search for coherence and community.[37]

The defining moment for many Catholics born before 1950 was the Second Vatican Council. Having been formed in a closed Catholicism and a deductive, apologetic theology, they were delighted to learn that they didn't have to have an answer for every question. They welcomed a less triumphal, more open Church and the opportunity to explore new issues. They were moved by *Gaudium et spes,* with its call to dialogue with the

37. Robert Schreiter, "Reflecting on Religious Life's Future," *Origins* 28/10 (1998) 167.

modern world, and many ultimately embraced what was seen as the council's progressive agenda.

The experience of many seminarians and religious today, however, is completely different. Most of them were born long after the council. The only Church they have known is the post Vatican II Church, in all its diversity and even confusion. Unlike earlier generations, raised on the *Baltimore Catechism,* they complain that they have not really been told what Catholics believe; nor have they been offered a coherent, articulate vision of their faith. They experience this as a loss; they are at a disadvantage with others better informed and want to get closer to our Catholic heritage. Thus they are much more interested in apologetics, not necessarily the approach of the "new apologists," but one rooted in the great tradition of the Church. The experience of other zealous young Catholics may be quite similar.

Why Catholics Leave the Church

A second problem with the new apologetics is that it doesn't seem to address the real problem of why Catholics are leaving their Church. As justification for his book Keating refers several times to the remarkable growth of the fundamentalist churches which in recent years have been gaining members, many of them former Catholics, at a surprising rate: "in many fundamentalist congregations a third, a half, or even a majority of the members once gave allegiance to Rome."[38] In Latin America the number of people who have left the Catholic Church to join evangelical and pentecostal communities in the last five years is estimated as high as forty million.[39] Though the reasons for their conversions are many, Keating asserts that "most converts have been influenced by arguments attacking 'Romanism'."[40] Later he says that Catholics who have returned to the Church from fundamentalism "almost universally declare that what kept them out of the Catholic Church was doctrine."[41]

Is it true, as Keating suggests, that Catholics who become fundamentalists are strongly influenced by issues of doctrine?

Though there is a need for more empirical data on why Catholics join other churches, some recent studies suggests that these departures are due to reasons far more complex than aggressive proselytism and anti-Catholic preaching. Allan Figueroa Deck argues that most Catholic commentaries on evangelical and pentecostal proselytism "have not sought to frame the

38. Keating, *Catholicism and Fundamentalism,* 14.
39. Cited in *The Tablet,* 250 (8 June 1996) 768–69.
40. Keating, *Catholicism and Fundamentalism,* 27.
41. Ibid., 342.

issue in its deeper social, cultural, and historical underpinnings. Catholic reflections on this trend have tended, rather, to be argumentative, to be a form of latter-day apologetics."[42]

A study prepared by the Center for Applied Research on the Apostolate (CARA) for the U.S. Bishops' Ad Hoc Committee on Proselytism observed that there "is little empirical evidence" to support the theory that one of the key reasons for the defection of new immigrants "is proselytism on the part of other denominations. Furthermore, there is some evidence, although sparse, that other denominations may be attracting Catholics because of their warm evangelization, rather than because of coercive techniques."[43] One of its recommendations was that "the Church admit, that while proselytism is occurring, there is a lack of evangelizing effort by the Church with newcomers."[44] More recently, William Shea suggests that the phenomena may be an occasion for some self-criticism on the part of the Catholic Church.[45]

It is important to ask the question, why is it that a significant number of Catholics are leaving the Church today for fundamentalist and evangelical communities. What needs are these communities addressing that the Catholic Church is not? Rather than simply criticizing them for proselytizing, Deck suggests a number of reasons for their success. Both Hispanic Catholicism and evangelical Christianity are premodern. Hispanic Catholicism is a popular Catholicism; it "is fundamentally a system of symbols with an exceedingly undeveloped formal doctrine or theology."[46] Communicated orally within the family, it is "almost totally" lacking rational articulation. Deck sees an "unanalyzed affinity" between this popular Catholicism—with its "concern for an immediate experience of God, a strong orientation toward the transcendent, an implicit belief in miracles, a practical orientation towards healing, and a tendency to personalize or

---

42. Allan Figueroa Deck, "The Challenge of Evangelical/ Pentecostal Christianity to Hispanic Christianity," in *Hispanic Catholic Culture in the U.S.: Issues and Concerns,* ed. Jay P. Dolan and Allan Figueroa Deck (Notre Dame, Ind.: University of Notre Dame Press, 1994) 415.

43. Eleace King, *Proselytism and Evangelization: An Exploratory Study* (Georgetown: CARA/Georgetown University, 1991) 16.

44. Ibid., 7.

45. William Shea, "Catholic Reaction to Fundamentalism," *Theological Studies* 57 (1996) 282.

46. Allan Figueroa Deck, "'A Pox on Both Your Houses': A View of Catholic Conservative-Liberal Polarities from the Hispanic Margin," in *Being Right: Conservative Catholics in America,* ed. Mary Jo Weaver and R. Scott Appleby (Bloomington, Ind.: Indiana University Press, 1995) 96.

individualize one's relationship with the divine"—and evangelical/pentecostal Christianity.[47]

Furthermore, Hispanic Catholics are particularly attracted to the emphasis on personal conversion and the smaller, more affective assemblies they find among evangelical and pentecostal Christians. At the end of his article Deck quotes William Read to the effect that the evangelization of Hispanic Catholics in the U.S. demands that one "abandon the cultural coldness, the systematized, privileged and secularized Christendom" of the mainline religions of North America.[48]

Both Deck and the CARA study suggest that the Catholic Church's failure to evangelize effectively may be more significant than anti-Catholic proselytism. Similarly, Shea points out that "the fundamentalist evangelization of Catholics is not matched in the Catholic literature, official and otherwise. The bishops show not the slightest sign of targeting fundamentalists for evangelization; their writings are defensive, not evangelistic."[49] Perhaps what the Catholic Church most needs is not more apologists, but more evangelists. This certainly seems to be the view of Pope John Paul II, who has repeatedly called the Church to a "new evangelization." In his 1998 apostolic exhortation "Ecclesia in America," given in Mexico City, he spoke of the many Catholics leaving the Church, calling for "prompt evangelizing efforts aimed at those segments of the people of God most exposed to proselytism." Specifically, this means a renewal of faith which would help "all the faithful to move from a faith of habit, sustained perhaps by social context alone, to a faith which is conscious and personally lived" (no. 73).[50] We will consider the Pope's call for a new evangelization in a later chapter.

Conclusions

One sympathizes with the evangelical concerns of these new apologists, their sense for the immediacy of God's self-revealing presence in Scripture, their desire to reaffirm, as Kreeft says, that an ordinary Christian can understand Scripture's true meaning without reading German theologians.[51] Thus it is important to acknowledge that these new apologists have some legitimate concerns; they are addressing some serious

---

47. Ibid., 412–22.
48. Ibid., 432.
49. Shea, "Catholic Reaction to Fundamentalism," 280.
50. John Paul II, "Ecclesia in America," *Origins* 28 (1999) 589.
51. Peter Kreeft, *Fundamentals of Christian Faith: Essays in Christian Apologetics* (San Francisco: Ignatius, 1988) 295.

questions in a not insignificant part of the Catholic community. Those who are converts bring new energy to the Catholic community. They have helped many Catholics, confused by the variety of opinions claiming to represent the tradition and by challenges from fundamentalist Christians, to find clear if simplistic answers to basic questions.

But an attempt to speak theologically on the basis of such an approach remains precritical. What emerges in their work is a new Catholic evangelicalism, but one which is burdened by the same difficulties as its earlier Protestant version; that is, it is biblicist, anti-hermeneutical, supernaturalist, has a univocal view of Church teaching, and pays little heed to historical development. Too often it falls into a type of fundamentalism, albeit a Catholic one. Because of their precritical approach, these new apologists appear unable to enter into a real dialogue with modernity, with the critical questions it raises for faith. An apologetics constructed on a precritical theology remains a house built on sand.

Thus the new apologists do not represent the best that Catholic theology has to offer. They will not be able to help contemporary Catholics develop a faith that is at once traditional and critical, able to withstand the challenges of secular modernity. Because of their hostility to contemporary theology and their noncritical method, they will not be able to help them come to terms with developments in the Church's teachings and changes in its life. Indeed, as Peter Huff of St. Anselm College observes, there is a separatist dimension to their critique: "Like dissident theologians engaged in 'internal emigration' and women-church feminists proposing a temporary 'space apart' from patriarchal church and culture, the new apologists locate authentic Catholicism in the diaspora, not the promised land of the National Council of Catholic Bishops or the U.S. Catholic Conference."[52]

Nor will they be able to help Catholics enter into the dialogue with culture so often called for by Paul VI and John Paul II. According to Bishop Stephen Blaire, the apologist needs to make "great efforts to engage intellectual capacity so that the gift of faith does not come off as absurd or as incompatible with reason."[53]

Contemporary theology makes every effort to dialogue with culture, using its philosophical and academic modes of discourse. But for an increasing number today, it seems much more secular than religious. Too often fragmented into various special interest theologies, it has become

52. Huff, "New Apologists in America's Catholic Subculture," 256.

53. Stephen E. Blaire, "The Apologetic Moment in Evangelization," *Origins* 26 (1997) 559.

separated from the life of the Church and the faith of ordinary believers, as we saw earlier. Thus, both apologists and professional theologians have much to learn from each other. The real challenge is learning how to give an account of our faith which is able to enter into dialogue with a post-modern world and still remain faithful to the tradition.

4

Scripture, Tradition, and Church

How does the Church address new problems, answer questions not faced by the first Christians or reflected on in their Scriptures? As the Church enters the third millennium, it faces many new questions that bear directly on its ability to carry out its mission of bringing salvation and reconciliation in Christ to a deeply divided human community.

Let us consider just a few of those questions. How will the Church find a new language for its faith, one that will bring the liberating message of the gospel to the millions of the poor and suffering who make up the majority of the world's people? How can the Church reconcile its faith and doctrine with scientific knowledge? Does its doctrine develop and change? Who decides on questions of doctrine?

What does the Church say to those who feel excluded from its life? What about women in the Church? Can they be called to ordained ministry? How can the Church learn to pray and name God in a more inclusive way? What does the Church say to those who are homosexual, not by choice, but from an orientation determined very early in their lives, perhaps even before birth? Are they to be told that the physical expression of their love in committed, exclusive relationships is sinful? What does it say to those whose marriages fail, and who seek new unions?

What does the Christian community say to the vast majority of human beings who belong to other religions? Is there salvation for those outside the Church? Are they excluded from God's grace if they do not make an explicit confession of faith in Jesus? Is grace to be found in their religious traditions? What grounds for dialogue exist between the different faiths?

What about human life questions such as abortion, the death penalty, the possibilities of genetic engineering? Do Christians have an obligation towards the environment?

Though the various Christian traditions have already arrived at different answers to many of these questions, all of them are challenged by doctrinal or moral questions such as these which they must seek to answer on the basis of their understanding of the gospel, Scripture, and their foundational traditions. For historical reasons Protestant Christianity has adopted a "Scripture alone" position. Yet as D. H. Williams, a Baptist minister teaching at Loyola University of Chicago argues, the doctrine of *sola scriptura* is not in the Bible and "cannot be rightly and responsibly handled without reference to the historic Tradition of the church."[1] He says that neither Luther nor Calvin rejected the authority of tradition, although they believed that it had to be regulated by Scripture. He attributes the assumption that the New Testament needs no external mediation—such as tradition or Church—to be clearly understood to the free-church perspective of the radical reformation. "It is this Free church perspective that tends to govern Evangelical ideologies of church and faith today."[2]

Catholic Christianity says "both/and," both "Scripture and tradition," or perhaps more accurately, "Scripture in tradition." As Vatican II said in its Dogmatic Constitution on Divine Revelation, *Dei Verbum,* "Sacred tradition and sacred Scripture form one sacred deposit of the word of God, which is committed to the Church" (DV 10). The position of Eastern Orthodoxy is similar. In this chapter we need to consider more carefully each of these interdependent elements, tradition, Scripture, and Church.

Tradition

For Catholicism, tradition in its most primary sense refers to the ongoing life of the Church itself. Yet too often the Catholic appeal to tradition is misunderstood as a separate "source" of revelation, a misunderstanding which has its origin in the language of the Council of Trent.

When the council fathers gathered at Trent in northern Italy, some of the Reformers were already maintaining that "Scripture alone" was sufficient for the Church's faith and life. As Avery Dulles has argued, the fathers were almost unanimously agreed that this was not enough: "Even if it contained all truth, Scripture could not be sufficiently understood without reliance on Tradition, enshrined in the works of the fathers and in ecclesi-

---

1. D. H. Williams, "The Search for *Sola Scriptura* in the Early Church," *Interpretation* 52/4 (1998) 364.
   2. Ibid., 358.

astical decisions."[3] We could go further and say that Scripture is always read within an interpretative tradition, even when this isn't acknowledged. The language, however, eventually adopted by Trent was to lead to misunderstandings that were to endure down to the time of Vatican II.

The decree on Scripture and Apostolic Tradition approved in 1546 said in reference to the Gospel of Jesus, "these truths and rules are contained in the written books and unwritten traditions which have come down to us" (DS 1501). Unlike the original draft, which had used the language of "partly . . . partly," suggesting that not all revelation was contained in Scripture, Trent's final text could be interpreted as holding that revelation was fully contained in either Scripture or tradition.

The council never used the expression "two sources of revelation." Unfortunately, this was the way that post-Reformation Catholicism usually interpreted Trent, so that the expression became part of the popular tradition. The first chapter of the initial draft for what became *Dei Verbum* was entitled "Two Sources of Revelation," though this draft was rejected and the expression does not appear in the final constitution.

Dei Verbum is essential for understanding how the Catholic Church understands the relation of Scripture and tradition as well as the whole question of revelation. It is one of the most important documents of the Second Vatican Council. Only this document and the one on the Church, *Lumen gentium,* are called "dogmatic" constitutions, meaning that they were promulgated with a formal doctrinal authority not given to the other documents.

A careful reading of *Dei Verbum* makes clear that the Catholic Church had moved from the propositional understanding of revelation, evident in the expression of Trent which reduces the Gospel to "these truths and rules" that we saw above, to a more personalist approach. The council sees revelation as God's self-communication in history which reaches its fullness in the person of Jesus, and through life in the Spirit offers men and women a share in God's own divine nature (DV 2). Revelation is not the communication of abstract truths expressed in dogmatic propositions or confessional formulas but rather God's deeds and words which reach a fullness in Jesus, the Word made flesh. In the council's understanding, revelation is personal rather than propositional, it is trinitarian in form, christological in realization, and historical in mediation. Furthermore, the Church's understanding of revelation continues to develop in history: "This tradition which comes from the apostles develops in the Church with the

3. Avery Dulles, *The Craft of Theology: From Symbol to System* (New York: Crossroad, 1996) 88.

help of the Holy Spirit. For there is a growth in the understanding of the realities and the words which have been handed down" (DV 8).

Thus Vatican II does not identify revelation with either Scripture or tradition as "sources." It is concerned to show how God's revelation in Jesus is transmitted through the life of the Christian community, the Church: "Sacred tradition and sacred Scripture form one sacred deposit of the word of God, which is committed to the Church. Holding fast to this deposit, the entire holy people united with their shepherds remain always steadfast in the teaching of the apostles, in the common life, in the breaking of the bread, and in prayers (cf. Acts 2, 42)" (DV 10). For Catholic Christians, tradition represents the Christian community's experience of God's grace and life present in Christ Jesus—its "faith" received, lived in discipleship, celebrated in worship and sacrament, expressed in written books, formulated in doctrines, and handed on.

Scripture

If tradition has such a profound resonance for Catholics, what role then does Scripture play? It might surprise many non-Catholic Christians how central Scripture is for most Catholics, how large a role Scripture plays in Catholic prayer and sacramental worship. The poet Kathleen Norris, a Presbyterian with a Benedictine spirit, observes that she has often found that the mainline Protestant congregations in which she has been asked to preach "are not asked to listen to the complement of Scripture readings that any Roman Catholic parishioner will hear at Sunday Mass—Old Testament, Epistle, Gospel, and responsorial psalm."[4] The revised Lectionary, which many Protestant congregations still do not use, is designed around a three-year Sunday and two-year weekday cycle of readings, to ensure that the four Gospels are read through sequentially and as much of the Bible as possible is read on a regular basis. The divine office or "Liturgy of the Hours," prayed publicly each day by monastic communities and in private by most priests, religious, and an increasing number of lay men and women, consists almost entirely of Scripture—psalms, canticles, and biblical readings.

The Bible is the book of the Church. It represents the faith experience of Israel and the primitive church expressed in writing. Catholics recognize that before there was a New Testament there were fully functioning churches, proclaiming their faith in the Risen Jesus, preparing candidates for baptism, celebrating the Eucharist, and appointing those variously

---

4. Kathleen Norris, *Amazing Grace: A Vocabulary of Faith* (New York: Riverhead Books, 1998) 189.

called presbyters or bishops to office with prayer and the laying on of hands. In Scripture the Church hears the voice of the Lord; it is God's word. The Church recognizes that these books were "committed to writing under the inspiration of the Holy Spirit." They are inspired writings, "sacred" Scriptures, and God is considered their principal author. It is more accurate to say that divine revelation is "contained and presented" in Scripture, rather than to identify Scripture with revelation (DV 11).

At the same time, the biblical authors are "true authors" (DV 11). Since, as *Dei Verbum* says, God speaks through human beings "in human fashion," biblical interpreters should carefully search out the meaning which the sacred writers had in mind. They must therefore pay attention to the "literary forms" used by the sacred author, the type or species of literature— "whether a text is history of one kind or another, or whether its form is that of prophecy, poetry, or some other type of speech" (DV 12).

The emphasis on paying attention to the literary form is extremely important. Biblical literary forms include poetry (epic, lyric, erotic, didactic, lamentations), patriarchal legends, court histories, law codes, prophetic oracles, fictional tales or stories, proverbs, apocalyptic visions, miracle stories, pronouncement stories, sayings of Jesus, liturgical formulas, parables, doxologies, and so forth. Most Catholics are able to recognize that a story, the deluge for example, is able to convey a divine truth just as much as an historical narrative.

The concept of biblical inerrancy (freedom from error) is one that divides Catholics from many evangelical or conservative Protestants. The concept is controversial. The Scriptures themselves do not specifically claim to be inerrant, but the idea that Scripture is true or trustworthy, variously expressed, is a constant in the tradition. Scriptures are true (Clement), perfect (Irenaeus), Scripture cannot contradict itself (Justin), does not deceive us (Hippolytus). According to Aquinas, it was heretical to say that anything false was contained in Scriptures. The actual term "inerrancy" is relatively recent. It is not found in any of the standard classical and medieval dictionaries and appears in English only as late as the nineteenth century.

But for conservative evangelicals and fundamentalists, inerrancy is the most basic of the "fundamentals."[5] It is generally understood to mean that the Bible is true in all its affirmations, even those in the areas of history, science, and attributed authors.[6] Thus, chapters 1–11 of Genesis are

5. Cf. Martin E. Marty, "Tensions Within Contemporary Evangelicalism: A Critical Appraisal," in *The Evangelicals,* ed. David F. Wells and John D. Woodbridge (Nashville: Abingdon, 1975) 180.

6. See Harold Lindsell, *The Battle for the Bible* (Grand Rapids, Mich.: Zondervan, 1976) especially 30–32.

taken as true, not just religiously but historically, all biblical miracle stories are considered as factual, and Peter is considered the author of the epistles that bear his name. But this approach runs into problems with historical evidence and raises many questions of interpretation. For example, are all parts of the Bible held to be of equal authority, even when they cannot be reconciled with each other? Or why do conservative Christians take so literally the few biblical passages dealing with homosexuality and ignore the clear teachings of Jesus about divorce and remarriage? In the final analysis, the notion of inerrancy held by most evangelicals is a philosophical rather than a biblical concept, maintained on confessional grounds.

Catholics are uncomfortable with this conservative understanding of inerrancy, not because they do not recognize Scripture as inspired, but because this approach so often leads to a fundamentalist or literalist interpretation of Scripture. They understand inerrancy as an effect of Scripture. It has to do more with the truth of the Bible as a whole than with any theory of verbal inerrancy. According to *Dei Verbum,* "the books of Scripture must be acknowledged as teaching firmly, faithfully, and without error that truth which God wanted put into the sacred writings for the sake of our salvation" (DV 11). The qualification "for the sake of our salvation" is key, for the contemporary Catholic Church does not identify Scripture with revelation, but sees it more as witness to God's revelation in history and in the person of Jesus.

The Catholic Church and Modern Biblical Scholarship

The Catholic Church was not always so open to an historical critical approach to the Bible. It was initially suspicious of the various critical, historical, and literary methods of investigating biblical texts (historical criticism, form criticism, redaction criticism, source criticism, text criticism) which had developed largely in the secular universities of Germany, heavily influenced by the rationalism of the Enlightenment. The so-called "Modernist crisis" at the beginning of the twentieth century left the Catholic Church even more fearful of the new scholarship.

Raymond E. Brown outlined three stages in which the Church gradually came to terms with modern biblical criticism.[7] In the first period, from 1900 to 1940, the Church resisted the biblical movement. Between 1905 and 1915 the Pontifical Biblical Commission (PBC), the Vatican commission charged with overseeing the use of the Bible in the Church, issued a number of decisions requiring Catholic scholars to hold positions

7. Raymond E. Brown, *Biblical Reflections on Crises Facing the Church* (New York: Paulist, 1975) 6–10.

that were being challenged by the new biblical scholarship. These included the substantial Mosaic authorship of the Pentateuch, the historical nature of the first chapters of Genesis, the view that the book of Isaiah was the work of a single author, that Matthew was the first Gospel written, that Luke/Acts was written in the 60s, and that Paul was the author of Hebrews.

The second period, from 1943 to 1970, saw a complete reversal of the Church's official position. The turning point came with Pope Pius XII's 1943 encyclical *Divino Afflante Spiritu,* instructing Catholic scholars to base their biblical translations on the original Hebrew and Greek texts, rather than the Latin, and giving them the green light to use the new methods of historical critical investigation. The Pope cautioned Catholics about being fearful of new ideas: "They must avoid that somewhat indiscreet zeal which considers everything new to be for that very reason a fit object of attack or suspicion."[8] In the following years, Catholic biblical scholarship began to flourish, while a number of church decisions and instructions showed that the attitude of the official Church was changing. In 1955, the secretary of the Pontifical Biblical Commission said that Catholic scholars now had "complete freedom" in regard to the conservative decrees of 1905–1915, except where they touched faith and morals.

In 1964, a year before the council's *Dei Verbum* appeared, the PBC published an "Instruction on the Historical Truth of the Gospels."[9] The instruction stressed that the gospels are not literal, chronological accounts of the words and deeds of Jesus, but the product of a three-stage development, moving from the ministry of the historical Jesus, through the oral preaching of the apostles, to finally the actual writing of the Gospels by the evangelists. According to this important instruction, words and deeds attributed to Jesus in the Gospels may really come from the preaching of the early Christian communities or from the particular evangelist who selected from, synthesized, adapted, and explicated the material he received. As the Instruction says, "the truth of the story is not at all affected by the fact that the Evangelists relate the words and deeds of the Lord in a different order, and express his sayings not literally but differently, while preserving (their) sense" (no. IX).

As more and more Catholic scholars were trained in the new methods and began to teach in seminaries and universities, the results of the new scholarship began to filter out to the Church at large. In 1972 Pope Paul

---

8. Pius XII, *Divino Afflante Spiritu,* no. 49; text from Catholic Truth Society (London, 1943).

9. A translation and commentary by Joseph A. Fitzmyer can be found in *Theological Studies* 25 (1964) 386–408.

VI restructured the Pontifical Biblical Commission by appointing for the first time internationally known Catholics scholars as members. But many conservative Catholics are still not comfortable with this change in the Church's position. They find it especially difficult to grasp that the gospel tradition went through different stages of development. Still, it is not necessary for them to toss out their red-letter New Testament editions. As a scholar as critical as Edward Schillebeeckx says, "a logion, though not actually spoken by Jesus, may be an utterance of the primitive Church, grounded in Jesus' inspiration and orientation."[10] Just because a particular saying does not represent the "very words" of Jesus doesn't mean it does not accurately reflect his teaching.

When Brown wrote about the Catholic Church and modern biblical scholarship twenty-five years ago, he predicted that the last period, from the 1970s to the end of the century, would see biblical criticism as well as historical studies having an impact on the Catholic understanding of doctrine. He also warned that the Church's magisterium would be all the more important as fundamentalist Catholics, unable to live with a more nuanced understanding of Catholic doctrine, would try to usurp the magisterium's authority by condemning theologians and positions with which they disagreed.[11] At the same time, liberal theologians sometimes use modern biblical studies to reject any Church tradition or teaching that cannot be shown as coming from the historical Jesus.

In spite of the controversy which we have been considering, the official Catholic Church remains committed to modern biblical scholarship. But it has also warned against reducing biblical scholarship simply to scientific exegesis. In 1993 the PBC published an important document entitled "The Interpretation of the Bible in the Church."[12] The document reaffirmed the necessity of historical-critical study of Scripture, giving it in the words of Joseph A. Fitzmyer "primacy of place."[13] It also evaluated both positively and negatively a number of contemporary hermeneutical theories as well as liberationist, feminist, and fundamentalist approaches.

Though it acknowledges that fundamentalism is correct in insisting on the divine inspiration of the Bible and the inerrancy of God's word, the PBC document warns that "its way of presenting these truths is rooted in

---

10. Edward Schillebeeckx, *Jesus: An Experiment in Christology* (New York: Seabury, 1979) 98.

11. Brown, *Biblical Reflections,* 13.

12. *Origins* 23/29 (1994) 497–524.

13. See Joseph A. Fitzmyer, "The Interpretation of the Bible in the Church Today," *Irish Theological Quarterly,* 62 (1996–1997) 89.

an ideology which is not biblical."[14] Among its errors, it mentions its failure to take into account the historical character of biblical revelation, its undue stress on inerrancy especially in what concerns historical events or supposed scientific truths, its tendency to confuse the final stage of the tradition (what the evangelists have written) with the first (the words and deeds of the historical Jesus), and its separation of the interpretation of the Bible from the tradition of the Church from which the New Testament developed. "Because of this, fundamentalism is often anti-church; it considers of little importance the creeds, the doctrines and liturgical practices which have become part of church tradition, as well as the teaching function of the Church itself."[15]

Part III of the document addresses the specific character of Catholic biblical exegesis. What distinguishes it is not some special method, but the fact that Catholic biblical interpretation always takes place within the living tradition of the Church. "Catholic exegetes approach the biblical text with a pre-understanding which holds closely together modern scientific culture and the religious tradition emanating from Israel and from the early Christian community."[16] Catholic exegesis uses the historical-critical method, but does so within the Church's understanding of its life and its faith. Implicit here is the Catholic conviction that truth is one, that human beings can come to know it, albeit partially, and that scientific and religious truths are complementary, not in contradiction to each other.

The PBC document cautions against reducing biblical scholarship to the scientific exegesis of historical documents and a study of their origins. A purely academic analysis risks failing to grasp the nature of the Bible as the word of God, addressed to the Church and to the present world. Therefore, Part IV, the final part of the document, considers how the Bible is interpreted in the Church's life. First, it calls for the "actualization" of the Bible, a "rereading" of the biblical message in the light of contemporary circumstances, a process already visible in the Bible itself. Secondly, the diverse places and cultures in which the Church lives call for an "inculturation" of the biblical message. Finally, it looks at how the Bible is used in the liturgy, in *Lectio divina* (the meditative reading of Scripture), in pastoral ministry, and in ecumenism.

The document concludes by reiterating that biblical interpretation will continue to require the use of the historical-critical method, as "the biblical writings cannot be correctly understood without an examination of the

14. Ibid., 509–10.
15. Ibid.
16. Ibid., 513.

historical circumstances that shaped them."[17] It notes that the "synchronic" approaches (rhetorical, narrative, semiotic, feminist, etc.) can also make a contribution. And it stresses again that biblical scholarship should avoid a kind of professional bias and remain a theological discipline, rooted in the great tradition. Thus it repeats in different ways the central message of the Second Vatican Council's *Dei Verbum,* that "sacred tradition, sacred Scripture, and the teaching authority of the Church . . . are so linked and joined together that one cannot stand without the others" (DV 10).

Church

According to *Dei Verbum,* the Church's teaching office, the magisterium, "is not above the word of God, but serves it, teaching only what has been handed on" (DV 10). But how does this interdependence of tradition, Scripture, and Church teaching authority come together in making doctrinal decisions? To answer this question, we need to consider first, how doctrines grow and develop out of the life of the Church, and second, the different kinds of doctrine and the nature of assent that is owed to each.

Development of Doctrine

Many Protestants and not a few Catholics think that teaching authority in the Catholic Church always operates from the top down. The pope as the head of the Church is the chief teacher and arbiter of doctrine. The pope and the bishops united with him constitute the Church's magisterium. Doctrinal questions are resolved simply by discovering what the magisterium has officially taught.

In reality, the process of resolving doctrinal questions is far more complex. *Dei Verbum* makes clear that the tradition continues to grow and develop, not just through the magisterium, but through the whole Church: "This happens through the contemplation and study made by believers . . . through the intimate understanding of spiritual things they experience, and through the preaching of those who have received the gift of truth" (DV 8). The magisterium has a special role to play in this process; indeed, this ability of the Church to clarify its beliefs through the decisions of the magisterium is one of the Catholic Church's greatest strengths. This capacity means that the Catholic tradition remains a living tradition, able to address new questions and arrive at new conclusions, sometimes reinterpreting previous teachings.

But this is not the work of the magisterium alone. The Holy Spirit works not just in the hierarchy; it is present in the entire Church. Accord-

17. Ibid., 524.

ing to Vatican II, to the definitions of the magisterium "the assent of the Church can never be wanting, on account of the activity of that same Spirit, whereby the whole flock of Christ is preserved and progresses in unity of faith" (LG 25). This is often referred to as the *sensus fidelium,* the sense of the faithful, clergy and laity together. The role of authority is to articulate what the Church—the whole Church—believes. Crucial to this process is an ecclesiological reality known as "reception."

Reception refers to the process through which doctrines, liturgical practices, and decisions of authority are "received" by local churches so that they become effective in the life of the Church as a whole. One can cite many examples. First of all, the Gospel itself, preached by the apostolic witnesses, was received by those who became the early Christians. The Church is a result of the reception of the Good News. The early Christian writings we refer to as the New Testament became authoritative expressions of the Christian tradition because in turn they were received by the early communities. But those communities also rejected other documents which claimed divine authority. The decrees and decisions of the great ecumenical councils were received by the churches. The gradual reception of the christological teaching of the Council of Nicaea (325), not without considerable opposition and even the loss of some churches from the communion of the church catholic, is a prime example of this. The practice of private, frequent confession of sins, brought to Europe by the Irish missionary monks in the sixth and seventh centuries, initially resisted by church authority, was gradually received. Finally it became the official and universal practice when the Fourth Lateran Council (1215) decreed that every Christian who committed a serious sin should confess it within the year.

There are also many examples of decisions of authority which were not received by the universal Church, and so did not become effective in its life. The Church did not receive the claim of Boniface VIII in the bull *Unam sanctam* (1302) "that it is absolutely necessary for the salvation of all men that they submit to the Roman pontiff" (DS 875). Similarly, the conciliarist teaching on the supremacy of a general assembly of bishops over a pope, expressed in the decree *Haec sancta* (1415) of the Council of Constance, was not received by the Church. Other examples might include Pope John XXIII's letter *Veterum sapientiae,* urging that Latin continued to be used in seminaries. One could ask if Pope Paul VI's encyclical on contraception, *Humanae vitae,* has been received by the Catholic faithful, or for that matter, if the recent attempts of the Vatican to declare the exclusion of women from ordination an infallible teaching has been received by the faithful.

It is also important to consider the modes of reception. A knowledge of church history shows that positions taught by the ordinary magisterium and held as Catholic doctrine—in some cases for centuries—have ultimately been changed, partly as a result of the development of doctrine, partly as a result of theological critique—a talking back to Rome on the part of theologians—and partly because of a lack of reception by the faithful. Examples from church history include teachings on the temporal power of the popes, the denial of salvation outside the Church, the conciliarist teaching of the Council of Constance, the Church's acquiescence in the practice of slavery, sanctioned by four ecumenical councils, and the justification and authorization of the use of torture for obtaining an admission of guilt.[18] Examples of more recent papal teachings modified or rejected by Vatican II include Pius IX's inability to find any truth or goodness in non-Christian religions, his condemnation of the proposition that Church and state should be separated, his denial of religious freedom as an objective right, as well as Pius XII's exclusive identification of the Catholic Church with the Mystical Body of Christ.[19]

What the practice of reception illustrates is that the Church cannot be conceived as an institution in which authority operates only from the top down. The Church cannot be divided into a "teaching church" and a "learning church," as popular Catholic theology was once wont to do.

Nor can it be understood on the basis of a congregationalist or egalitarian ecclesiology, where all authority comes from the base. Rather the Church functions as a communion of different elements, the bishops as official teachers, theologians with their scholarship, prophetic voices, and the faithful in whom the Spirit is also at work. The Church's essential nature is organic; there is an element of interdependence or shared responsibility in its very nature.

Even in the case of the extraordinary papal magisterium, its so-called "infallible definitions," the papal magisterium cannot operate independently of the Church. In the only two examples of infallible papal definitions—the dogma of the Immaculate Conception defined by Pius IX in 1854, and that of the Assumption, defined by Pius XII in 1950—in both cases the definitions were made only after a process of consulting the faithful through a polling of the bishops.

18. See Luis M. Bermejo, *Infallibility on Trial: Church, Conciliarity and Communion* (Westminster, Md.: Christian Classics, 1992); also *Rome Has Spoken: A Guide to Forgotten Papal Statements, and How They Have Changed Through the Centuries,* ed. Maureen Fiedler and Linda Rabbens (New York: Crossroad, 1998).

19. J. Robert Dionne, *The Papacy and the Church: A Study of Praxis and Reception in Ecumenical Perspective* (New York: Philosophical Library, 1987).

Thus doctrine grows out of the life of the Church, its understanding of Scripture, its prayer and worship, its reflection on the Christian mysteries, and its theology. Though we cannot avoid expressing our faith in abstract doctrinal statements, they remain, even while true, one or more levels removed from the mysteries they seek to express.

Doctrine and Dogma

The Catholic Church distinguishes between doctrine and dogma. Dogmas are teachings or doctrines considered to have been divinely revealed and proclaimed with the Church's highest authority. They constitute a "rule of faith." They can be reinterpreted, reformulated, expressed more adequately, but they cannot be reversed and so are called "irreformable." Dogmas include the articles of the creed, the solemn teachings of the ecumenical councils, and the *ex cathedra* (infallible) pronouncements of the ordinary papal magisterium.

Doctrines (from the Latin *doctrina,* "teaching") are beliefs that the Church has recognized as official teachings, whether from Scripture, councils, or the papal magisterium. The fathers of the Second Vatican Council were careful to distinguish between infallible exercises of the magisterium and what are generally referred to as teachings of the ordinary (or "noninfallible") magisterium. Dogmas are owed a "submission of faith" (LG 25). To dissent from a dogma places one outside the communion of the Church.

Doctrines are teachings of the ordinary magisterium, whether papal or conciliar; the faithful are obligated to accept them with a "religious submission *(obsequium religiosum)* of will and of mind" (LG 25). But precisely because they are not proclaimed infallibly, the possibility of error cannot be excluded. Therefore doctrines can not only be reinterpreted; they can also be "reformed" or changed, as occasionally happens in the life of the Church as we have seen. Theology has an important role to play in probing the tradition and seeking always more adequate ways to express the Church's faith in language.

An Expanded Authority?

In the last ten years, faced with some questions that won't seem to go away, the Vatican has taken a number of steps to strengthen and perhaps expand the authority of the ordinary magisterium.

The first came in 1989 in the revised "Profession of Faith," published by the Congregation for the Doctrine of the Faith (CDF). Pope Paul VI's 1967 Profession of Faith, following Vatican II, had said "I firmly embrace and accept all and everything which has been either defined by the Church's solemn deliberations or affirmed and declared by its ordinary magisterium concerning the doctrine of faith and morals."[20] Implicit here is the traditional distinction between solemn or dogmatic teachings, whether divinely revealed or having a necessary connection with revealed truth (the so-called "secondary object" of infallibility), and "doctrines," ("non-definitive," "non-infallible") teachings of the ordinary magisterium.

The revised profession introduces a distinction between three different kinds or levels of truth, each with a different degree of assent. The first level involves those divinely revealed and therefore irreformable truths which are "proposed by the Church—whether in solemn judgment or in the ordinary and universal magisterium." They are owed an assent of faith. The second level we will consider below. The third level concerns the teachings of the ordinary (noninfallible, non-definitive) magisterium, which are owed a religious submission of will and intellect (cf. LG 25).

It is the second level that has become a subject of controversy. It includes whatever is proposed by the Church "definitively with regard to teaching concerning faith and morals." These teachings one must "firmly accept and hold."[21] The 1990 "Instruction on the Ecclesial Vocation of the Theologian" added a clarification on the kind of teaching involved. These are truths "which, even if not divinely revealed, are nevertheless strictly and intimately connected with revelation" and must be "firmly accepted and held" (no. 23).[22] Here the "secondary object" of infallibility has emerged as a separate category.

But how can a teaching be said to be "definitively proposed"? According to Francis A. Sullivan, they can be recognized "either by the fact than an ecumenical council or a pope has pronounced a 'solemn judgment' about it, or by the fact that the whole college of bishops, together with the pope in their ordinary exercise of teaching authority, have consistently proposed the same point of doctrine as 'definitively to be held'."[23] But they were not considered to require an "assent of faith," as such teachings are not declared to be divinely revealed.

In his 1994 apostolic letter *Ordinatio sacerdotalis* Pope John Paul II stated: "I declare that the church has no authority whatsoever to confer priestly ordination on women and that this judgment is to be definitively

---

20. Cited in "Profession of Faith and Oath of Fidelity," *Origins* 18/40 (1989) 663–64.

21. Ibid.

22. "Instruction on the Ecclesial Vocation of the Theologian," *Origins* 20 (1990) 122.

23. Francis A. Sullivan, *Creative Fidelity: Weighing and Interpreting Documents of the Magisterium* (New York: Paulist, 1996) 16.

held by all the church's faithful."[24] A number of commentators were confused by the kind of authority claimed for this teaching, since it was not recognized as something that had been infallibly defined. Archbishop Rembert Weakland said, "As a bishop I will have to ponder what the phrase *this judgment is to be held definitively,* means in terms of its demands on the faithful. This terminology is not traditional in the Catholic Church."[25] Sullivan commented that claims were being made for this document that "have never before been made about any document of ordinary papal teaching."[26]

The year 1995 saw a second step, represented by several efforts on the part of Rome to attribute infallibility to certain teachings of the ordinary universal magisterium. In his encyclical *Evangelium vitae,* Pope John Paul II specifically condemned murder, abortion, and euthanasia. In a "Note" on the encyclical's doctrinal weight, Sullivan argued that there are good reasons for thinking that the Pope intended to invoke in regard to these condemnations the infallibility attributed by Vatican II to the ordinary and universal magisterium, even if Cardinal Joseph Ratzinger stopped short of saying that they met the conditions for infallibility.[27]

Then on November 18, in response to certain doubts about the authority of the Pope's letter *Ordinatio sacerdotalis,* the Congregation for the Doctrine of the Faith published a statement declaring that the teaching reiterated by the Pope belongs to the deposit of faith and has been infallibly taught by the ordinary and universal magisterium.[28] Yet it was not clear to many theologians that the Church's criteria for judging that a teaching of the ordinary and universal magisterium was infallibly taught had been fulfilled. Canonist Ladislas Örsy argued that the CDF's response simply conveyed the interpretation and authority of the congregation; it did not effect the weight of the apostolic letter.[29] Francis Sullivan, after reviewing the criteria, found that a question remained as to whether or not the bishops of the Church were unanimous in teaching that the exclusion of women from ordination to the priesthood is a divinely revealed truth. His conclusion: "Unless this is manifestly the case, I do not see how it can be

24. John Paul II, *"Ordinatio sacerdotalis," Origins* 24 (1994) 49–52, no. 4.

25. *Origins* 24/4 (1994) 55.

26. Francis A. Sullivan, "New Claims for the Pope," *The Tablet* (18 June 1994) 769.

27. Francis A. Sullivan, "The Doctrinal Weight of *Evangelium vitae," Theological Studies* 56 (1995) 564.

28. CDF, "Response to *'Dubium,'" Origins* 25 (1995) 401.

29. Ladislas Örsy, "The Congregation's 'Response': Its Authority and Meaning," *America* 173/19 (1995) 5.

certain that this doctrine is taught infallibly by the ordinary and universal magisterium."[30]

On June 30, 1998, Pope John Paul II's apostolic letter "To Defend the Faith" inserted certain penalties into the Code of Canon Law for those who dissent from "definitive" but noninfallible teachings.[31] In an accompanying declaration from the CDF, Cardinal Ratzinger warned that those who dissent from truths such as these would be in a position of *"rejecting a truth of Catholic doctrine and would therefore no longer be in full communion with the Catholic Church."*[32]

Naturally theologians are very concerned, not just about the threatened "just" penalties, but also about their ability to continue their work. Archbishop Tarcisio Bertone, secretary for the CDF, denied that anyone intended to "put the brakes" on theological research and discussion. He acknowledged that the letter "touches theologians, but not to limit them in their freedom to research," as long as the "dissent and debate" does not touch "definitions of the faith"[33] But that is precisely where there remains some debate. Can a teaching which is neither revealed nor clearly established as infallibly proclaimed be said to belong to "definitions of the faith" simply because authority declares that it is to be held "definitively"? This is what has caused confusion. Richard P. McBrien commented that the Pope and the CDF "have been smudging the theological distinction between infallible and noninfallible teachings."[34]

So many questions remain unanswered. On a practical level, theologians wonder how the penalties might be applied; will they come from the Vatican, or will the bishops be required to enforce them? On a theological level, theologians and some bishops question what seems to be an expansion of magisterial authority beyond the way it was understood by Vatican II. Many wonder how an issue as sensitive today as the ordination of women, both for the Catholic Church itself and in its ecumenical relations with other churches, can be closed to discussion, without a careful consultation with the bishops themselves who with the pope constitute the magisterium. It is confusing to many to argue that the matter has been set forth in-

30. Francis A. Sullivan, "Guideposts From the Catholic Tradition," *America* 173/19 (1995) 6.

31. John Paul II, *"Ad Tuendam Fidem,"* *Origins* 28/8 (1998) 113–16.

32. Joseph Ratzinger, "Commentary on Profession of Faith's Concluding Paragraphs," *Origins* 28/8 (1998) 117, italics in original.

33. "Teaching-Bertone," Catholic News Service, 1 July 1998.

34. Richard P. McBrien, "The Vatican's Unnecessary Roiling of the Waters on Dissent," *Los Angeles Times* (6 July 1998) B,5.

fallibly by the ordinary magisterium when the bishops themselves have not been permitted to discuss it.

On deeply divisive questions, what constitutes the faith of the Church should not be judged too hastily or answered simply by appealing to authority. Nor should scholarly research and discussion, without which careful decisions cannot be made, be forbidden. There is too much at stake.

Conclusions

Both Catholics and Protestants from the mainline churches understand that the Bible is always read within a tradition. As Baptist theologian Timothy George has written, "for all their rhetoric about 'Scripture alone,' Protestants in the sixteenth century, and Baptists in the seventeenth and eighteenth, not only affirmed the dogmas of the early Church in the language of the ancient creeds, but also added to these classic statements their own particular confessions of faith."[35]

But many American Protestants have inherited the free church perspective of the radical reformation; too often they have turned the scripture principle into an absolute warrant for private interpretation. At the end of his article about searching for *sola scriptura* in the early church, D. H. Williams asks, "How can American Protestants simply gloss over a thousand years of Church history and believe that they know how to interpret the Bible or that they alone possess the truth?"[36] One has only to look at the innumerable divisions in the ecclesial traditions stemming from the Reformation or "surf" the UHF dial in the late evening to see the consequences of the free church Protestant separation of Scripture from the living tradition of the Church. One television preacher, quoting liberally from Hal Lindsey, sees in Ezekiel a prediction of a Russian invasion of Israel or the Common Market as the ten-nation confederacy that is a forerunner of the antichrist prophesied in the book of Daniel. Another urges political support for the nation of Israel against the Palestinians on the basis of "biblical prophecy." Such is the unhappy legacy of private interpretation.

For Catholics, tradition is not a source in the distant past; it is the dynamic process by which the Church lives from its originating events and through its on-going encounter with the Lord rearticulates the implications of life in Christ for today and tomorrow. But there are parameters. Scripture is the tradition of Israel and the apostolic Church concretized in writing. It is the *norma non normata,* the norm that is superior to all others for Christian theology.

35. Timothy George, "Southern Baptist Ghosts," *First Things* 93 (May 1999) 19.
36. Williams, "The Search for *Sola Scriptura*," 364.

But Scripture does not stand by itself. As the book of the Church, it is always read and interpreted within the Church's living tradition. Doctrines may develop in the tradition beyond what is explicitly contained in Scripture. The magisterium has the task of authentically interpreting the Word of God, whether written or handed on. Yet it is not above the Word of God, but serves it (DV 10).

Thus for Catholics, Scripture, tradition, and Church go together. They cannot be separated one from another without giving up the unity of the Church.

5

Sexuality Morality

The theological divisions that we have been considering so far are important issues for theologians and for those on the left or right wings of the Church. But for the vast majority of American Catholics, it is questions of sex and gender which most often are cause for controversy and even for dissent. Thomas Reese, S.J., editor of *America* magazine, says that the battle about sex is over: "On questions of birth control, masturbation, premarital sex, divorce and remarriage, the hierarchy has lost most of the faithful."[1] According to Andrew Greeley, Catholics in the last two decades have moved to more liberal positions on these and other issues like abortion, family gender roles, and public roles of women.[2] Archbishop Rembert Weakland says that the Catholics who represent the largest group in his archdiocese seem to ignore much of the Church's teaching on sexuality and make their own decisions on many of these questions, using common sense.[3] According to James Davidson's study, published by *Our Sunday Visitor,* 80 to 90 percent of Catholics registered in parishes (i.e., "practicing" Catholics) reported that central doctrines such as the incarnation, resurrection, Trinity, and eucharistic real presence were important to their faith. But only a minority agreed with the Church's sexual and reproductive ethics. Those saying that a particular action was "always wrong"

1. Thomas J. Reese, "2001 and Beyond: Preparing the Church for the Next Millennium," *America* 176/21 (1997) 11.

2. Andrew Greeley, "Polarized Catholics? Don't Believe Your Mail!" *America* 176/6 (1997) 13.

3. Rembert Weakland, "Reflections for Rome," *America* 178/13 (1998) 12.

dropped to 41 percent on homosexual actions, 39 percent on abortion, 33 percent on premarital sex, and only 9 percent on artificial birth control.[4]

Even so, sexuality remains an extremely sensitive issue because it touches the most personal and intimate areas of our lives. Questions of divorce and remarriage, sexual relations outside of marriage, birth control, and in particular, homosexuality—these questions of sexual life and practice continue to trouble the Church. How do Catholics approach these questions today, and what guidance can the Church provide? We will consider some of these questions in this chapter. First, we will consider Catholic moral theology, particularly as it has been interpreted by Rome. Second, we will look at the contemporary debate over the morality of sexual relations between committed homosexuals as a concrete example of traditional moral theology. Third, we will ask, what might a biblical morality have to say about our sexual lives? Finally we will attempt to draw some conclusions about integrating law and gospel.

Moral Theology

Traditional Roman Catholic moral theology is based on obedience to the divine will, known through Scripture and by reflection on the moral law inscribed on the human heart. This law as grasped by natural reason, with its awareness of obligation, of the good to be done and evil to be avoided, is called the "natural law." In its full meaning, the natural law is the internal grasp of the order of creation as it is expressed in the natural and spiritual nature of the human person. In regard to sexuality this analysis resulted in concrete norms or "rules," based on the meaning of the human body-person. Acts such as masturbation, premarital or extramarital sexual relations, homosexual relations, contraception, direct sterilization, and artificial insemination were all seen as frustrating the normative expression of sexuality within marriage and/or the intended purpose of the sexual faculties. Thus they were judged to be intrinsically evil and morally unacceptable.

In more recent history many Catholic moral theologians have adopted a position known as proportionalism. Proportionalism presupposes that in an imperfect and sinful world there is often an ambiguity in our moral choices, and therefore some acts are difficult to describe as simply evil. What is important in any given act is that evil should not be intended as an end, and if tolerated, there be some proportionate good to be achieved.[5]

---

4. James D. Davidson, et al, *The Search for Common Ground: What Unites and Divides Catholic Americans* (Huntington, Ind.: Our Sunday Visitor, 1997) 200–01.

5. See for example Richard A. McCormick, "Ambiguity in Moral Choices," in his *Doing Evil to Achieve Good* (Chicago: Loyola University Press, 1978) 7–53.

One of the first to broach this issue was Peter Knauer, S.J., who raised the question of proportionality in the context of the principle of double effect.[6] The name proportionalism comes from its emphasis on the proportionate good intended. For example, Charles Curran has argued that while heterosexual marital relations remain the ideal, an individual homosexual might well come to the moral conclusion that a permanent homosexual union is the best way for him or her to achieve a truly human life. Obviously it is better than homosexual promiscuity.[7]

Thus proportionalism is often described as teleological, goal directed, or "revisionist," as opposed to a "traditionalist" or "deontological" ethics, which holds that certain actions are intrinsically evil in themselves, regardless of their consequences. Because of proportionalism's emphasis on goal or consequence *(telos),* its critics have identified it with utilitarianism or consequentialism, a charge the proportionalists reject. Others accuse it of subjectivism, which one author admits is not so easily dismissed, as some people will not be able to find the objectively right thing to do in a given situation.[8]

Veritatis splendor

Pope John Paul II, a former professor of ethics at the Catholic University of Lublin in Poland, is very familiar with the debate in Catholic moral theology. He has done much in his writing to develop a positive theology of the body. His 1993 encyclical *Veritatis splendor* represented a strong reaffirmation of the traditional teaching of Catholic moral theology that the negative precepts of the natural law are universally valid (no. 52).[9] He specifically rejected proportionalist and consequentialist ethical theories for maintaining "that it is never possible to formulate an absolute prohibition of particular kinds of behavior" that would in every case be in conflict with the moral values indicated by reason and revelation (no. 75). In the clearest terms, the Pope reaffirmed the existence of "intrinsically evil acts," actions that are always wrong in themselves apart from the circumstances and intention of the one acting (no. 80), affirming that the existence of such intrinsically evil acts is affirmed by Scripture (no. 81).

6. Peter Knauer, "The Hermeneutic Function of the Principle of Double Effect," in *Readings in Moral Theology: No. 1,* ed. Charles E. Curran and Richard A. McCormick (New York: Paulist, 1979) 1–39.

7. Charles E. Curran, *Catholic Moral Theology in Dialogue* (Notre Dame, Ind.: Fides, 1972) 217.

8. Bernard Hoose, *Proportionalism: The American Debate and Its European Roots* (Washington: Georgetown University Press, 1987) 141.

9. John Paul II, *Veritatis splendor, Origins* 23/18 (1993) 297–334.

How are these absolute prohibitions known? They are known from God's revelation in Scripture, "the living and fruitful source of the Church's moral doctrine" (no. 28) and from rational reflection on "the nature of the human person" (no. 50). The Pope rejects any view that denies "a specific and determined moral content, universally valid and permanent" to divine revelation as well as any denial that the magisterium has "a specific doctrinal competence" with regard to particular moral norms (no. 37).

Vatican I taught that the pope could under certain circumstances teach infallibly concerning faith and morals. Most Catholic theologians would not exclude the possibility of the magisterium infallibly defining some doctrine regarding morals as revealed or as necessary for the defense of revealed truth, the so-called "secondary object" of infallibility. But there remains a question as to whether the Church has actually done either of these things.[10]

Francis Sullivan suggests that John Paul II in *Veritatis splendor* has laid the groundwork for making the claim that the Church's traditional moral teaching is infallibly taught "by identifying the authority of the magisterium on moral issues with its authority to interpret divine revelation. This would insert all moral issues into the primary object of infallibility and make it that much easier to claim that many traditional Catholic moral doctrines have been infallibly taught by the ordinary universal magisterium."[11] But could this effort to see traditional Catholic moral teaching on specific issues as divinely revealed stand up to critical analysis? Let us consider a practical example, homosexual relations.

A Practical Example

Following the approach of Thomas Aquinas, the official Catholic position on homosexuality takes as its ultimate moral norm "right reason," based on the order given in nature. Since that order calls for the depositing of the male seed in the vagina of the female, homosexual acts are considered "sins against nature" in that they violate this biological finality.[12] Thus, like much of its moral theology, the Catholic position on homosexuality is based primarily on natural law reasoning, supported with some appropriate biblical texts.

Though the Bible seems to presuppose the immorality of homosexual acts, the biblical evidence is not as conclusive as might be thought. Homo-

10. Francis A. Sullivan, "Infallible Teaching on Moral Issues?" in *Choosing Life: A Dialogue on Evangelium Vitae,* ed. Kevin Wm. Wildes and Alan C. Mitchell (Washington: Georgetown University Press, 1997) 78.

11. Ibid., 83.

12. Curran, *Catholic Moral Theology in Dialogue,* 198.

sexual acts are condemned in both the Old and the New Testament. Yet on closer examination, it is not so clear that the biblical authors were condemning the physical expression of love between homosexuals who are in committed and exclusive relations. First, the concept of a homosexual orientation was unknown until modern times. Second, in the judgment of many biblical scholars the biblical condemnations are aimed at something other than homosexual acts considered in themselves.

The condemnations in Leviticus (18:22; 20:13), part of the Old Testament Holiness Code, are aimed at preserving ritual (rather than moral) purity. Several are associated with idolatry, specifically with participation in idolatrous worship by consorting with male (and female) prostitutes (Deut 23:18), a common practice in the ancient Near East (1 Kgs 14:24; 15:12). Other passages are concerned with violating the duty of hospitality through homosexual rape (Gen 19:4-8), or with pederasty (1 Cor 6:9-10; 1 Tim 1:10). Romans 1:24-31 is more difficult; here Paul is clearly talking about homosexual relations in themselves. But the fact that he describes both men and women as *giving up* natural relations and *choosing* homosexual ones suggests that he did not understand homosexuality as a condition.[13]

Although the *Catechism of the Catholic Church* repeats the traditional teaching that "homosexual acts are intrinsically disordered" and can never be approved (2357), it also acknowledges that a homosexual orientation is not a matter of choice (2358). Thus the Church recognizes that sexual orientation is something that is determined very early in a person's life, perhaps even prior to birth. But if this is so, then, many ask, why is the Church not able to move beyond its traditional condemnation, particularly when it seems to be based not on biblical revelation but on a philosophical reflection on human nature? Why can't homosexual acts be seen in a broader context, one that includes not just the act but the quality of the relationship as well? And they wonder if it is realistic to insist that the only moral possibility for homosexuals is celibacy.

Would it not make more sense to encourage homosexuals to form stable and lasting relationships, even if those relationships might sometimes lead to sexual expression? Many Catholic theologians, following the traditional teaching recently reaffirmed by Pope John Paul II in *Veritatis splendor,* would answer no, on the basis of the principle that negative precepts of the natural law are universally valid. Others like Charles Curran

---

13. See Vincent J. Genovesi, *In Pursuit of Love: Catholic Morality and Human Sexuality* (Wilmington: Michael Glazier, 1987) 262–73; also Victor Paul Furnish, "The Bible and Homosexuality," in Jeffrey S. Siker, ed. *Homosexuality in the Church: Both Sides of the Debate* (Louisville: Westminster John Knox, 1994) 18–35.

in his "theory of compromise,"[14] would answer yes, even though they would continue to maintain that homosexual relations fall short of the ideal. John McNeill, a former Jesuit, goes even further. Rejecting Curran's position, McNeill argues that homosexual relations could be morally justified if they were expressive of a genuinely constructive human love.[15] Thus there remains considerable difference among Catholics on this question.

Towards a More Biblical Morality

The fathers of the Second Vatican Council recognized the need for a renewal of Catholic moral theology. The Decree on Priestly Formation points to Scripture as "the soul of all theology." Though it did not reject the place of speculative reason, so valued by scholasticism, the decree noted that "Special attention needs to be given to the development of moral theology. Its scientific exposition should be more thoroughly nourished by scriptural teaching" (OT 16). Moral theologians like Bernard Häring and Josef Fuchs called for a moral theology that placed the concept of moral law in a broader framework that was biblically based, Christ-centered, and relational rather than individualistic.[16]

But placing greater emphasis on the biblical tradition raises a number of hermeneutical problems. How is the Bible to be interpreted? One approach takes the text itself as the ultimate norm. But this approach runs into the dilemma of the literalist, who argues as did the Southern Baptist Convention in 1998 for the submission of wives to husbands on the basis of texts such as Ephesians 5:22-24. Yet those who claim divine authority for this text rarely do the same for the demand that slaves be obedient to their human masters—implying a divine legitimation of slavery—which comes just a few verses further on (Eph 6:5) as part of the same passage. On what grounds is the first part of the passage seen as God's will and the other rejected? Similarly, biblical passages against homosexuality will be read as absolute ethical norms, while modern biblical criticism, seeing them in their historical context, understands them as concerned with idolatrous worship or pederasty.

Another approach is to find the principle of interpretation in the history behind the text. This is the approach of Elisabeth Schüssler Fiorenza who argues that "the locus of revelation is not the androcentric text but

14. Curran, *Catholic Moral Theology in Dialogue,* 216–18.
15. John J. McNeill, *The Church and the Homosexual* (New York: Next Year Publications, 1985) 34.
16. See Bernard Häring, *The Law of Christ,* 3 vols. (Westminster, Md.: Newman, 1961–1966); Josef Fuchs, *Human Values and Christian Morality* (Dublin: McGill and Macmillan, 1970).

the life and ministry of Jesus," the egalitarian reality of the early Christian movement which lies behind the text.[17] The Jesus Seminar represents a similar approach; it rejects much of the New Testament tradition in favor of its own reconstruction of the historical Jesus.

A third approach locates the principle of interpretation in the ongoing tradition of the Church. The Scriptures represent a crystallization of the primitive tradition of the early Christian communities, and they continue to be read within this community of faith. The Church guards, proclaims, and interprets Scripture in light of its faith (cf. DV 10). This approach takes seriously the need to use historical critical scholarship to discover the historical meaning of the text; it places the primary emphasis on the meaning intended by the author. Recognizing the literary form of a particular passage, for example, distinguishing a Greco-Roman household code (or rules for domestic order) such as the Ephesians passage referred to above from New Testament ethical instruction or *parenesis,* avoids the kind of literalism which turns incorporated cultural material into God's revelation. At the same time, the ongoing life of the Church provides a critical principle for understanding or reinterpreting problematic passages. However, as Lisa Cahill notes, "The crucial question whose answer is so elusive, is exactly how and to what degree the original meaning or its historical reference acts as a critical standard of subsequent interpretation."[18]

Does the Bible have much to say about human sexuality? On the one hand, the Bible should never be reduced to a collection of moral prohibitions. Nor should the New Testament be seen as presenting a specific sexual ethic; it represents an interpretation, instruction, and exhortation on the meaning of life in Christ and in his Spirit. On the other hand, it is not true that the New Testament simply speaks in general terms about loving one's neighbor. What can we say specifically about Scripture and sexuality?

First, Scripture presupposes the primacy of the union of man and woman in marriage.[19] Genesis teaches that sex is for procreation (1:28) and mutual love (2:18-24). The physical love of man and woman is frankly celebrated in the Song of Songs, an erotic poem. Jesus presupposed the divine institution of marriage and affirmed its permanence (Matt 5:31-32). Paul echoes this teaching. Even though he had not known the historical Jesus, Paul is aware of his teaching on the permanence of marriage (1 Cor 7:10).

17. Elisabeth Schüssler Fiorenza, *In Memory of Her: A Feminist Reconstruction of Christian Origins* (New York: Crossroad, 1985) 41.

18. Lisa Sowle Cahill, *Between the Sexes: Foundations for a Christian Ethics of Sexuality* (Philadelphia/New York: Fortress/Paulist, 1985) 33.

19. Philip S. Keane, *Sexual Morality: A Catholic Perspective* (New York: Paulist, 1977) 15.

He recognizes marriage as a charism, a gift of the Spirit for the building up of the Church (1 Cor 7:7). The intimate union of husband and wife in marriage is a symbol or sign of a great mystery *(mysterion),* the union of Christ and the Church (Eph 5:31-32). Marriage is thus seen as sacred, though it is interesting to note that both Paul (1 Cor 7:10-16) and Matthew (5:32; 19:1-2) admit exceptions to Jesus' prohibition of divorce and re-marriage in particular cases.

Second, the Bible does condemn certain types of sexual acts that are considered deviant from the general norm of heterosexual, monogamous, permanent marriage. Lisa Sowle Cahill offers the following list:

> Adultery (Lev 20:10; Gen 39:9; Prov 2:17; Sir 23:16-21; Exod 20:14; Deut 5:18; Mark 7:22; Matt 5:28; 15:19; 1 Cor 6:9); fornication (Sir 42:10; Deut 22:13-21; Lev 19:29; *porneia* or "sexual immorality" as including fornication, Mark 7:21; Matt 15:19; 1 Cor 5:9-11; 7:2; 2 Cor 12:21; Gal 5:19; Eph 5:3, 5), homosexual acts [but note what we said above] (Lev 18:22; 20:13; Rom 1:27; 1 Cor 6:9).[20]

Clearly the New Testament does not consider sexual conduct as unrelated to the life of faith in the Christian community.

One sees this particularly in Paul. Though he is sometimes portrayed as stressing justification by faith over the demands of ethical living, his letters show considerable concern for chastity and holiness of life. They stress chastity, including chastity in sexual relations. At Corinth, where a member of the community has been living in an incestuous relationship with his stepmother, he instructs the community to excommunicate the offender (1 Cor 5:1-3). And in response to others in the community who were attempting to justify sexual license on the basis of their understanding of Christian freedom, he argues that since a union already exists between the Christian and Christ, any sexual union should reflect the holiness of this prior relationship. In this way he sketches the outline for a theology of sexual relationships (1 Cor 6:12-20).

This same concern for the holiness of the life of the baptized is evident in an earlier, rarely commented upon, passage in the first letter to the Thessalonians. In the NRSV translation, Paul tells the Thessalonians: "For this is the will of God, your sanctification: that you abstain from fornication; that each one of you knows how to control your own body, in holiness and honor" (1 Thess 4:3-4). The phrase translated here as "control your own body" *(skeuos ktasthai)* means literally "to acquire his vessel,"

---

20. Lisa Sowle Cahill, "Humanity as Female and Male: The Ethics of Sexuality," in *Called to Love: Towards a Contemporary Christian Ethic,* ed. Francis A. Eigo (Villanova, Pa.: Villanova University Press, 1985) 87.

but there is some debate about how it should be translated. According to the *New Jerome Biblical Commentary* the expression probably reflects a Hebrew idiom meaning "to take a wife," but "some commentators interpret Paul's metaphor in the sense of 'keeping one's body (or more specifically, the male organ) under control.'"[21]

Finally, on an even deeper level, one must always ask in regards to questions of sexual conduct, what does it mean to be a disciple of Jesus. To be a Christian is not just to have faith in God and faith in Jesus. It is to be a disciple, to hear the call of Jesus, to follow him in the service of his Kingdom. Discipleship in the Gospels covers every aspect of our lives; it means a personal and often costly following of Jesus.

First, it shapes a person's attitude towards property and wealth. The archetypal story is the call of the rich man, a talented man who has kept all the commandments. Jesus, however, challenges him by saying, "You are lacking in one thing. Go, sell what you have, and give to the poor and you will have treasure in heaven; then come, follow me" (Mark 10:21). Mark adds that his face fell, and he went away sad, because he had many possessions. And Jesus, looking at his disciples, comments: "How hard it is for those who have wealth to enter the kingdom of God" (Mark 10:24).

Second, discipleship affects one's human and erotic relationships. In the Sermon on the Mount Jesus warns that lust cannot be the basis of our relationships; even to look at a woman with lust is already to have committed adultery with her in one's heart (Matt 5:28). He affirms the permanence of marriage, as we have seen, and teaches that some are called to celibacy for the same of the Kingdom of heaven (Matt 19:12). Thus it is something of a cop-out to argue that Jesus says nothing specific about how we should live our sexual lives. One finds the same themes emphasized in the early Christian communities, which taught inclusion and sharing across traditional status boundaries against a culture which emphasized class difference, the patriarchal family, and its accumulation of property. In this context, Lisa Cahill sees as "dangerously countercultural" early Christianity's aversion to divorce, its downplaying of procreation and family ties (Mark 3:31), its mild advocacy of equality in marriage (1 Cor 7:2-5), its identification of female worth in roles outside of marriage, as in the story of Mary and Martha, and particularly its idealization of celibacy.[22]

---

21. Raymond F. Collins, "The First Letter to the Thessalonians," *The New Jerome Biblical Commentary,* ed. Raymond E. Brown, Joseph A. Fitzmyer, and Roland E. Murphy (Englewood Cliffs, N.J.: Prentice Hall, 1990) 777.

22. Lisa Sowle Cahill, *Sex, Gender, and Christian Ethics* (Cambridge: University Press, 1996) 151.

Third, discipleship gives a new meaning to love. Disciples are called to love others with a love that is sacrificial and without conditions or limits. Christians are called to love not just their friends, but their enemies as well. They are to share whatever they have with others (Luke 6:30). Nowhere is the ideal of discipleship more clearly expressed than in John's Gospel where Jesus says: "This is my commandment: love one another as I love you. No one has greater love than this, to lay down one's life for one's friends" (John 15:12-13).

Fourth, discipleship changes the way one understands success and personal fulfillment. Success is measured not in terms of achievement, wealth, or positions of power, but in terms of service. In the kingdom leaders are to be the last of all and the servants of all (Mark 9:35).

Finally, discipleship calls one to enter deeply into Jesus' paschal mystery, his passage through death to life. At its heart is what the Christian tradition came to call the *imitatio Christi,* the imitation of Christ.

Integrating Law and Gospel

Thus the Gospel suggests that Christian discipleship should inform both our interpersonal lives and our social lives. Sexual morality is concerned with the appropriate expressions of the drive for intimacy, love, and generativity which plays such an important role in our interpersonal relations. Unfortunately, Catholic moral theology, developed to assist priest confessors in identifying sins and assigning their proper penance, too often became legalistic in its expression.[23] Cut off from dogmatic and spiritual theology and influenced by Trent's emphasis on the juridical role of the confessor, moral theology became overly focused on sin. On questions such as birth control, masturbation, and homosexual relations, its natural law ethics relied far more on a philosophical analysis of human nature than on biblical revelation. Thus many moral theologians today are seeking to integrate this natural law ethics with the gospel.

If Catholics today are making up their own minds on questions of sexuality, it does not appear that their lives or their relationships are the better for it. Statistics indicate that Catholics fail in their marriages, have abortions, practice artificial contraception, or are engaged in premarital sex at about the same rates as their non-Catholic neighbors. According to Andrew Greeley, single Catholics are "significantly less likely to have been chaste during the last year than single Protestants (34 percent versus 43 percent).[24]

23. See John Mahoney, *The Making of Moral Theology: A Study of the Roman Catholic Tradition* (Oxford: Clarendon, 1987).

24. Andrew Greeley, *Sex: The Catholic Experience* (Allen, Tex.: Tabor, 1994) 113.

Greeley does not think this means that Catholics have become promiscuous or that they have bought into a sexual permissiveness; rather most seem to be faithful to their regular partners. His conclusion is that "Catholic laity—single and married—seem to have chosen an ethical perspective which emphasizes the bonding function of sex, while the leadership of the Church still emphasizes the procreative function, however much it may have changed the rhetoric of this emphasis."[25]

Yet this more relaxed ethic for single Catholics, even if it does not in most cases lead to promiscuity, does not seem to make them better prepared for or contribute to the success of their marriages. Nor is it true that those who live together before marriage, and thus become familiar and comfortable with each other, are more likely to avoid an unhappy marriage. According to seven recent studies, couples who live together prior to marriage have higher divorce rates than those who do not:

> A U.S. survey of 13,000 adults found that couples who lived together before marriage were one third more likely to separate or divorce within a decade. . . . A Canadian national survey of 5,300 women found that those who cohabited were 54 percent more likely to divorce within fifteen years. And a Swedish study of 4,300 women found cohabitation linked with an 80 percent greater risk of divorce.[26]

The high rate of divorce for those who have been sexually active before marriage suggests that there may be more wisdom in the Church's sexual ethic—with its emphasis on genital sexuality finding its appropriate expression in a loving and exclusive relationship, open to new life—than is generally acknowledged.

One thing overlooked today, particularly by the arguments of some expressions of feminism, is that the sexual nature of men and women seem to be different. Helmut Thielicke argues that a man invests far less of himself in the sex act and "is not nearly so deeply stamped and molded by his sexual experience as is the case with the woman."[27] Man's tendency is polygamous, while the woman's is monogamous. It is much more difficult for the woman to separate the physical from the personal; she "is the one who receives, the one who gives herself and participates with her whole being, is profoundly stamped by the sexual encounter."[28] Even if a man

25. Ibid., 118.
26. David G. Myers, *The Pursuit of Happiness* (New York: Avon Books, 1993) 162.
27. Helmut Thielicke, *The Ethics of Sex*, trans. John W. Doberstein (New York: Harper and Row, 1964) 81.
28. Ibid., 84.

might live polygamously without apparently doing serious harm (which would mean conceiving man in isolation from woman), for a woman to do so would be to do damage to her self as feminine. From this, Thielicke concludes to an ethic, based not primarily on natural law, but on the implications of the gospel.

> Once we see that Christian *agape* regards this "existence-for-the-other-person" as the foundation of all fellow humanity, and that it regards man as being determined by his neighbor, it becomes apparent that under the gospel there is a clear trend toward monogamy. Because the wife is a "neighbor," the husband cannot live out his own sex nature without existing for her sex nature and without respecting the unique importance which he himself must have for the physical and personal wholeness of the feminine sex nature.[29]

More recently Wendy Shalit has argued convincingly that the contemporary denial of sexual difference, making women in sexual matters completely equal to men, has been a disaster for women. Instead of liberating them, it has resulted in an increase of sexual harassment, stalking, rape, and a tragic loss of self-esteem manifested in anorexia, bulimia, and self-mutilation.[30]

Arguments such as this are usually considered unacceptable today as they presuppose a difference between men and women rooted in their respective natures. One hears similar arguments from Pope John Paul II. But it is interesting how often pastoral experience bears them out. Most pastoral counselors and priests who have done marriage counseling are painfully aware how deeply a woman, once she gives her love to a man, remains bound to him, even when he has long abandoned her. Sexuality for her is much more relational than physical. Nor are such counselors ready to agree that the Church should develop a more tolerant sexual ethic for young people, even given the fact that marriages are often delayed until they are in their late twenties or early thirties. In his book *American Catholic,* Charles R. Morris observes that almost all the priests he talked to, including the liberal ones, rejected the idea. Several gave as their reason the way that women in particular were being exploited.[31] In Greeley's words, "sex without public commitment is fraught with dangers of deception, self-deception and exploitation, particularly of women by men."[32]

---

29. Ibid., 90.

30. Wendy Shalit, *A Return to Modesty: Discovering the Lost Virtue* (New York: The Free Press, 1999).

31. Charles R. Morris, *American Catholic* (New York: Random House, 1997) 365.

32. Andrew Greeley, "Sex and the Single Catholic: The Decline of an Ethic," *America* 167 (1992) 343.

The Church's moral teaching on the permanence and exclusivity of marriage, the importance of its being open to children, the proper context for sexual expression, the sanctity of life—no matter how offensive to contemporary liberal culture—is deeply rooted in the Bible and the Christian tradition. It is owed an *obsequium religiosum,* that religious submission of mind and will that the council said must be shown to the teachings of the ordinary magisterium (LG 25). To ignore this teaching is not merely to trivialize the meaning of sexual relationships. It is to cause heartbreak and suffering, especially for the woman, and to diminish the likelihood that either partner will ultimately be successful in marriage, adding to a culture of dysfunctional families, abandoned spouses, and children in broken homes.

But the questions raised by those who have been marginalized by the Church's teaching—those in second marriages without annulments, gays and lesbians trying to live in faithful relationships, those unable to afford or support more children—will continue to trouble the Church. This is where the current debate is joined, not about the existence of moral norms rooted in our human nature, but over the question of whether those norms are universally applicable.

In the final analysis, these difficult cases often come down to a decision of conscience. Although the Church has not hesitated to interpret the teachings of Jesus for our lives, it has always stressed the primacy of conscience. This is as true for our sexuality, as it is for any other aspect of our lives. The Second Vatican Council describes conscience as "the most secret core and sanctuary" of an individual where he or she is alone with God (GS 16). But it is important to remember that conscience is not an inner voice or a subjective feeling; it is the specific, practical judgment made in a particular case after a careful consideration of the situation in light of our moral reasoning.

A person is bound to follow his or her conscience. However conscience is not autonomous; it can be in error, even if this is not always recognized or acknowledged in our subjective and relativistic culture, which believes that there is no standard of right and wrong other than the personal judgment arrived at by each individual. Lack of maturity, simple ignorance, an uncritical conformity to cultural values, the inability to separate desire or self-interest from what pertains to the common good, not making the effort to discover the truth—any or all of these can contribute to an erroneous conscience. The obligation to form one's conscience is a serious one.

The Church assists in this process. Christian life should be informed by the gospel, interpreted within the community of faith, not by the values of a particular culture. The Church hands on the gospel through its Scripture, its tradition, and through its magisterium or official teaching office. At the same time, a vision based on the gospel tradition should never blind one to compassion and recognition of the uniqueness of the individual.

Conclusions

Catholics may pay less attention to Church "rules" today, but the loss of a credible magisterial voice in regard to sexual conduct is only to be regretted. Many young Catholics grow up ignorant of their own tradition and can expect little help from a culture which both glorifies and trivializes sex, counseling only that it be safe and consensual. As Thomas Reese has suggested, the effects of the sexual revolution have not been all that liberating: "with the changes in sexual attitudes have come increases in pornography, extramarital sex, date rape, sexual activity among children, illegitimacy, abortion, adultery, divorce and sexually transmitted diseases, to say nothing of broken hearts."[33]

Though the New Testament does not develop a complete sexual ethics, it presupposed the moral teaching of the Jewish tradition out of which it developed. Furthermore, there is sufficient evidence to show that the authors of the New Testament books did not ignore sexual conduct or consider it irrelevant to the life of the Christian community. Indeed, the social and sexual values of the early Christians were often considered threatening to the culture in which they lived.

Catholic moral theology, based on the concept of natural law, has attempted to combine God's revelation in Scripture with a philosophical reflection on human nature. But in regard to questions such as artificial contraception, masturbation, artificial insemination, and relations between those who are constitutionally homosexual, philosophical reflection has played the primary role. This needs to be more readily acknowledged. For example, given the judgment of many biblical scholars that the Bible is unaware of the concept of sexual orientation and that its condemnations of homosexual acts seem more concerned with idolatrous worship and the exploitation of minors, it would be more honest to admit that the Church's position is based primarily on philosophical reasoning. It might need to be rethought in light of a modern understanding of sexual identity.

The question of divorce and remarriage seems a more difficult problem, given the clear teaching of Jesus. But as we saw earlier, both Paul and Matthew admit in particular situations of exceptions to his prohibition of divorce and remarriage.

---

33. Thomas J. Reese, "2001 and Beyond," 11.

One of the lessons of postmodernist thought is that our understanding of God, world, and self is not as open to neat, rational comprehension as we once thought. Without accepting the postmodernist view that all our systems of meaning are socially constructed on the basis of issues of power, race, and gender, and therefore suspect, we can recognize that they are perhaps not as universally explanatory as we once thought. There are places where our worldviews and systems of meaning crack and break down. There are areas of darkness in our own lives. It is in these areas of darkness, where each person is alone with God, that the traditional teaching of the Church on the primacy of conscience comes into play.

At the same time, the Church's teaching on the permanence of marriage, the importance of its being open to new life, the proper context for sexual expression, and the sanctity of life—even if unpopular—is a message that needs to be heard. The effects of sexual irresponsibility are all around us. Discipleship asks of the Christian considerably more.

6

Eucharist and Liturgy

The Eucharist is at the center of the Catholic experience of Church. When we break the bread and share the cup in memory of Jesus, we come to recognize the risen Jesus present in our midst. And in our *koinonia* in his body and blood, we become more fully Church, the body of Christ, his visible presence in the world.

This eucharistic sense of Church is still strong among Catholics today. And yet our experience of Eucharist has changed as a result of a new emphasis in our eucharistic theology and the changes in our eucharistic practice in the years since the Second Vatican Council. If those changes have been generally for the good, it is true that there are very different opinions in the Catholic community today about what good eucharistic theology demands, about what constitutes good liturgical practice, about how we celebrate, participate, and show reverence for this basic mystery from which the Church lives.

Nothing could be more concrete than the opinions present among us today. Should we stand or kneel during the Eucharistic Prayer? What about extraordinary eucharistic ministers? Can lay people serve as eucharistic ministers when there are concelebrating priests present? What about concelebration; is it still appropriate? Should Communion be received in the hand or on the tongue? Does one genuflect or bow on entering the church, and what about those who don't seem to make any sign of reverence? Why has Benediction all but disappeared from the life of the Church? What about eucharistic devotion, adoration of the Blessed Sacrament? Where should we place the tabernacle, and how should we arrange our liturgical space? How should we worship on Sundays, given the increasing shortage of priests? Many dioceses have introduced priestless communion services, called officially "Sunday Worship in the Absence of a Priest" (SWAP)[1] and the U.S. Bishops' Committee on the Liturgy plans to study the practice of having such services on weekdays. At the same time, other bishops have argued—with good reason—that such services are being confused by many with the Eucharist itself, and are insisting instead on Sunday Word services without the distribution of Communion.

I find considerable difference in approaches among my students. A few refuse to serve as eucharistic ministers, the more sophisticated ones citing documents such as the recent Vatican Instruction, "Some Questions Regarding Collaboration of the Nonordained Faithful in the Sacred Ministry of Priests."[2] Some kneel during the consecration and Eucharistic Prayer, though our practice is for the community to remain standing. Others genuflect in approaching the priest or eucharistic minister for Communion.

Other students are eager to serve as eucharistic ministers, and find a liturgy where their participation is excluded in favor of the ordained too clerical. They welcome the opportunity to share their own faith experience in "reflections," sometimes given in place of the homily. Others, particularly our women religious and graduate students, are happy to preside at paraliturgical services, an evening prayer or a lay-led Communion service. Many want to see more lay preaching. So there is a great deal of diversity.

Recently Milwaukee Archbishop Rembert Weakland has distinguished three groups with different agendas for liturgical renewal or reform. The first group wants to return to the pre-conciliar, Tridentine usage; the second or "restorationist" group wants to go back to the council documents; and the third wants to continue to improve the reform.[3] The presence of Catholics with these competing agendas makes it difficult for the Eucharist to be the sacrament of unity that the Church since St. Paul understands it to be. Too often it has become one more sign of division.

In this chapter I want to look at our liturgical practice today from several perspectives. First, we need to look briefly at *why* the liturgical renewal of the council was so necessary, which means that we need to consider some less-than-happy medieval developments. Second, we will consider some of the principles for liturgical renewal articulated by the council. Third, in a more practical reflection, we can ask, "where are we today,

---

1. Congregation for Divine Worship, *Directory for Sunday Worship in the Absence of a Priest,* 1988; see NCCB edition (New York: Catholic Book Publishing Company, 1994).

2. *Origins* 27/24 (1997) 397–409.

3. Rembert G. Weakland, "Liturgy and Common Ground," *America* 180/5 (1999) 8.

looking at the "lights and shadows" of our present liturgical life. Finally, we will briefly consider some unresolved issues.

Medieval Developments

There are many ways to trace the medieval developments which had the unhappy effect of separating the priest from the people and the people from the liturgical action. I would like to use here a seminal article first published in 1960 by Joseph Jungmann, S.J., one of the pioneers of the modern liturgical movement. The article, with the impossible Germanic title, "The Defeat of Teutonic Arianism and the Revolution in Religious Culture in the Early Middle Ages,"[4] explores a number of "shifts of accent and changes of viewpoint" in the five hundred years separating the death of Gregory I (604) from the time of St. Bernard of Clairvaux (1090–1153). These shifts resulted in a revolution in the understanding of both Church and liturgy which has left its mark down to our own time.

Contrasting early Christian and early medieval religious culture, Jungmann highlights a shift from an essentially corporate understanding of the liturgy—what we might call today an understanding based on the theology of the liturgical assembly—to one which had largely detached the priest from the congregation. In the early Christian age, he writes, "the liturgy is essentially *corporate public worship* in which the people's Amen resounds, as St. Jerome tells us, like a peal of heavenly thunder; there is a close connection between altar and people, a fact constantly confirmed by greeting and response, address and assent, and acknowledged in the verbal forms of the prayers, above all by the use of the plural."[5] Yet five hundred years later, the priest's role had been detached from that of the congregation. The spiritual action in the canon of the Mass or Eucharistic Prayer, now said silently by the priest, was to remain hidden from the people; the later prohibition of translating the canon into the vernacular represents a hardening of this attitude. Similarly the altar was moved further away from the people, and receiving Holy Communion became something of an exception, reserved for special feast days.

Jungmann points to a number of factors in this shift. First, the Easter motif which had dominated the early liturgy gave way to an increasing emphasis on the crucified Christ, and thus, the eucharistic sacrifice, rather than the glorified Lord. From the eleventh century, the crucifix became a central object on the altar and from the twelfth, artistic representations of

---

4. Joseph Jungmann, *Pastoral Liturgy* (New York: Herder and Herder, 1962) 1–101.

5. Ibid., 2.

the crucifixion became the dominant subject represented on the wall behind the altar. Another shift was from the predominance of mystery in the early period, and hence, the objective and corporate, to a Teutonic emphasis on the subjective and the individual. With this new emphasis, moralism and a sense of personal unworthiness replaced a sense for baptismal holiness, and the reception of the Eucharist declined, to be replaced with a contemplation of the sacrament from a distance. Still another was that the spiritual notion of the Church, often imaged as a woman, as virgin and mother, gave way to an emphasis on the Church's juridical-hierarchical structure, so that by the late middle ages the Church had become predominantly an earthly, sociological entity.

What emerged from these shifts and changes was an institutional understanding of Church, a sacral model of priesthood, and a eucharistic theology which saw the Mass primarily as a sacrifice offered to God, not in thanksgiving, but to obtain benefits. Though the Council of Trent clarified points of doctrine disputed by the Reformers, it also solidified these changed accents, making them to a considerable degree a matter of church doctrine. In the following Baroque period, the Church's liturgical life entered into a period of stability in which the consecration increasingly became the formative center of Catholic worship. But this was an unfortunate development. In Jungmann's words: "The measure in which the sacramental Presence becomes central, is also the measure in which truly sacramental thinking fades out."[6] In other words, the starting point became, not what the Church did liturgically, but rather doctrine, here, the doctrine of the real presence, often expressed even today in the unhappy expression, "the miracle of transubstantiation." An abstract, second-level theology, had taken the place of liturgy.

Vatican II initiated a massive shift in the self-understanding of the Church and in its liturgical consciousness which has yet to be completely appropriated by the faithful—both lay and ordained—or fully expressed in the Church's life and structure. But in the thirty-five or so years which have passed since the end of the council, the Church has experienced at least three major shifts in the area of ecclesiology and liturgy which have reversed to a considerable extent the "dissolution at the heart of ecclesiastical and liturgical life" which Jungmann had uncovered in his analysis.

First, the Church has moved from a monarchical, institutional ecclesiology to a collegial, communal one based on the biblical image of the People of God and the ecclesial concept of communion. Second, its understanding of priesthood has changed from a sacral model based on the con-

6. Ibid., 88.

cept of sacred power, specifically, the priest's power to "confect the Eucharist," to a representative, sacramental one. Finally, having rediscovered the communal character of the liturgy, the Church is struggling to find ways to move from a liturgy centered on the actions of the priest to one which takes much greater account of the liturgical assembly.

Vatican II and Liturgical Renewal

The long struggle for the renewal of the liturgy, carried on by scholars like Jungmann and many others, finally bore fruit at the Second Vatican Council. The council's Constitution on the Sacred Liturgy *(Sacrosanctum concilium)* called for the renewal of the liturgy in the life of the Church and for the specific revision of the various liturgical rites. Using the Constitution on the Liturgy, the subsequent documents and revised liturgical books, we can summarize a number of principles which have guided the post-conciliar liturgical renewal of the Catholic Church.

1. *Full, Active Participation.* According to the Constitution, "Mother Church earnestly desires that all the faithful be led to that full, conscious, and active participation in liturgical celebrations which is demanded by the very nature of the liturgy" (SC 14). This is the foundational principle of the liturgical renewal. The people should be encouraged to participate "by means of acclamations, responses, psalmody, antiphons, and songs, as well as by actions, gestures, and bodily attitudes" (SC 30).

2. *Simplification of the Rites.* "The rites should be distinguished by a noble simplicity; they should be short, clear, and unencumbered by useless repetitions" (SC 34). Those who have studied the history of the liturgy know how much the rites have been encumbered over the centuries by additions and repetitions. The liturgy might be compared to a grandparents' attic, which had accumulated all sorts of family treasures, but then became over-crowded. For example, the Missal of Pius V, mandated by the Council of Trent, multiplied symbols added over the centuries. The Mass had become a ballet of ritual gestures. Every rubric was significant, binding under pain of sin, from the more than twenty-five signs of blessing and the five different kinds of bows made by the priest in its course, to the joining of his thumb and forefinger after the consecration, to the exact number of inches separating his hands when extended in prayer. The council fathers wanted to simplify all this, so that the meaning of the liturgical symbols would be more obvious.

3. *Recovery of the Theology of the Liturgical Assembly.* In the liturgical language of the first millennium, it is clear that the entire assembly

celebrates the Eucharist. The General Instruction for the revised Roman Missal (1970) has returned to this view; so has the *Catechism of the Catholic Church.* Under the title, "The celebrants of the sacramental liturgy," the Catechism states, "It is the whole community, the Body of Christ united with its Head, that celebrates" (1140). Thus, the priest is more appropriately referred to as "presider" than "celebrant." But the challenge still remains to find appropriate ways to make our liturgies more participative, so that the assembly's role in the celebration might be more clearly expressed.

4. *Diversity of Liturgical Ministries.* This is a corollary of the theology of the liturgical assembly. An assembly-centered liturgy should manifest a diversity of liturgical ministries; thus, not just a priest-presider, but also lectors, cantors and music ministers, communion ministers, servers, and perhaps a deacon (cf. SC 28, 29). When roles are appropriately shared and all have a part, the result is a liturgy which gives better expression to the liturgy as the celebration of the entire community, not just of the priest.

5. *Liturgical Inculturation.* The council opened the way for developing styles of liturgical celebration more at home in various cultures, thus for a greater inculturation of the liturgy. Perhaps one of the most significant steps of the council, however hesitant at first, was allowing for the use of vernacular languages (SC 36). But the constitution on the liturgy goes much further, providing "Norms for Adapting the Liturgy to the Genius and Traditions of Peoples" (Section D).

The section begins with a statement that could stand as a principle: "Even in the liturgy, the Church has no wish to impose a rigid uniformity in matters which do not involve the faith or the good of the whole community" (SC 37). It goes on to speak of preserving intact the "spiritual adornments" and gifts of different peoples as long as they are not contrary to the faith, of allowing for variations and adaptations to different groups, regions, and peoples in revising the liturgical books and structures of the rites, leaving the decision in these matters to the regional episcopal authority. Only those cases are reserved to the authority of the Holy See where a more radical adaptation of the liturgy is proposed. Some progress has been made on different continents, for example, introducing drums and native dances in Africa or occasionally a more eastern posture in India. In 1988 the Congregation for Worship approved a Mass text for use in Zaire, but insisted that it be called "Roman Missal for Use in the Dioceses of Zaire."[7] Other efforts of national episcopal conferences have been stymied

7. *Notitae* 24 (1988) 455–72.

by higher authority; witness the efforts of the American bishops to introduce a moderate inclusive-language Lectionary.

Where We Are Today

When we pause to realize how much our identity as Catholic Christians has been molded and shaped by the Eucharist as well as to think about the considerable change our Church has been through in the more than thirty-five years since the end of the council, it might be good to ask, where are we today?

There have been many positive developments. The revised Lectionary, with its three-year cycle of readings, and the increasing emphasis on the importance of the homily, even at daily Mass, has restored Scripture to its central place in the liturgy. The liturgy for most of the rites and sacraments has been happily renewed (penance remains an exception here). As liturgist J. Leo Klein observes, "One almost never hears complaints about the reformed liturgy of funerals, with its emphasis on hope and final victory. Few would want to see the anointing of the sick return to extreme unction. The rediscovery of the adult catechumenate has carried us far beyond *Father Smith Instructs Jackson.*"[8]

To a considerable degree we have recovered a sense for the theology of the assembly. Even our language has changed. We don't talk about "saying" or "hearing" Mass, "fulfilling our Sunday obligation," and one rarely hears today—unless one is reading the most conservative sources—once hallowed expressions such as "the holy sacrifice of the Mass" or "the miracle of transubstantiation." Our language is now more communal and participative. We speak of the Mass using terms such as "celebration," "liturgy" "presider," "community," "proclamation of the word," and "homily." We are used to a multiplicity of liturgical ministries, with women ministers and altar servers of both sexes. People who thirty years ago were changing lanes at Communion so they could receive from a priest are today eucharistic ministers themselves. Thus our liturgical celebrations have been to a considerable extent declericalized.

In spite of the old cliché that "Catholics don't sing," I think that the use of music and song in contemporary Catholic liturgy sets a high standard for the rest of the Church. We have come a long way from the days when liturgical music meant an opening song, an "offertory" hymn, a Communion hymn, and a recessional. I have often been impressed with the way that liturgical music in many of our celebrations flows with and carries the liturgical action, providing a kind of dialogue of song joining the

8. J. Leo Klein, "Sources of the Christian Spirit," *America* 180/21 (1999) 9.

lectors, the congregation, and the presider. We move easily from presidential greeting to sung penitential rites, from lessons to sung or chanted responsorials, to alleluias which greet and answer the gospel, to sung responses to the universal prayers, even to Eucharistic Prayers sung by the presider, sometimes with antiphonal congregational responses. Not that all of this is done in every liturgy, or that it is always done well, but many of our celebrations are carried by a dialogue of ritual action, prayer and song that becomes a genuine dialogue between the assembly, its president, and the Lord. On the other hand, I've been in churches of other traditions where the liturgical action was interrupted at various points for long hymns, usually with five or more verses, or in silent congregations where the singing was the work exclusively of soloists or small choirs. In some cases, it was simply recorded.

At the same time, there have been some significant losses. If our liturgy has been declericalized, made more inclusive, it has also been to a considerable extent desacralized. If we've moved beyond the wild experimentation of the 1970s, some of our liturgies are still too informal, too "chatty," and overly verbal, with several welcomes, the three Sunday readings, various commentators introducing or explaining them, and a homily. There is little time for silence and contemplation of the mysteries celebrated, either before the liturgy begins or at points during it. And some of our "liturgical" music sounds more like it came from a cocktail lounge or an Off-Broadway theater. The council did not intend to jettison the great musical tradition of the Church; it specifically called for the retention of the great "treasure of sacred music" (SC 114), including Gregorian chant and sacred polyphony (SC 115), as well as for congregational singing (SC 118).

More serious is the fact that a considerable number of young Catholics seem to have little familiarity with what Catholics have called the "real presence" of Christ in the Eucharist. On a recent quiz I asked a class of first-year university students, almost all Catholics, "what is understood by the eucharistic doctrine of the 'real presence'?" The majority could not adequately answer the question. They pointed to a vague presence of Christ without mentioning either the bread and wine or the community becoming the body of Christ. Some simply spoke of "accepting Jesus" into their lives or their hearts. One said it referred to the "presence of God in everyday life." Perhaps we have so emphasized the Mass as a celebration of community that questions like this are difficult. The loss of eucharistic Benediction from the devotional life of the Church could also be a factor here. Archbishop Weakland raises questions about posture, genuflections, the placement of the tabernacle, and care for the Eucharist after Mass. He asks, "Have the very forms liturgical renewal has taken diminished belief in and respect for the real presence?"[9]

These shifts in emphasis could also explain what often appears to be a lack of reverence and loss of a sense of the sacred. I've seen Catholic undergraduates approaching communion with chewing gum in their mouths or baseball caps on their heads. Thus we need to find a middle ground between exaggerated signs of reverence which isolate the bread and wine from the ritual action of the sacramental meal, on the one hand, and on the other, an informality and lack of reverence inappropriate to the mystery we celebrate.

A final problem results from a disproportionate emphasis on the role of the liturgical assembly. This risks reducing the meaning of the liturgy to a purely horizontal dimension. Some overlook the role of the ordained presider; they conclude that the priest is simply a delegate of the community, with the result that some communities have taken it upon themselves to authorize their own presiders. But this is to sever the ancient bond between eucharistic presidency and apostolic office, a connection evident at least since Ignatius of Antioch at the beginning of the second century. To deny this link is to ignore the nature of the Church as an ordered community.

Unresolved Issues

Beyond the lights and shadows of the liturgical renewal of the last thirty-five years, there are a number of unresolved issues which will continue to be discussed. How do we show proper reverence in our eucharistic celebrations? Should the assembly stand or kneel, receive the host in the hand or on the tongue? Has an emphasis on Christ's presence in the assembly replaced the traditional belief in his real presence in the bread and wine?

We are divided by the question of liturgical posture. Many argue that having the congregation kneeling while the priest stands during the Eucharistic Prayer introduces a subtle difference in status between presider and assembly. If the whole assembly offers the liturgy, then all should assume the same posture, as they would if they were gathered around a table. Others argue that the congregation—they probably wouldn't say assembly—should kneel out of reverence for the Christ's presence "on the altar." Several years ago at the annual meeting of the U.S. bishops, a proposal to allow the assembly to stand during the Eucharistic Prayer was, regrettably in my opinion, rejected by a narrow majority. It's interesting

9. "Liturgy and Common Ground," 10.

to note that at the Council of Nicaea in 325, the fathers felt it necessary to add a canon forbidding the novel practice of kneeling during the Eucharistic Prayer (can. 20). But genuine reverence seems far more important than uniformity of practice.

If Catholics are united in their sense for Christ's unique presence in the Eucharist, just how that presence is to be explained continues to divide them. This was evident recently in Mother Angelica's critical reaction to Cardinal Roger Mahony's pastoral letter "Gather Faithfully Together: A Guide for Sunday Mass." The letter of course is on the liturgy, not on the doctrine of the real presence, taken in isolation. In discussing Holy Communion, the Cardinal notes "the wonder and thanksgiving Catholics feel toward the body of Christ—the consecrated bread and wine, and the Church. Both have the same name."[10]

What is the precise relation between the presence of Christ in the gifts of bread and wine and his presence in his body, the Church? In the New Testament, the emphasis is on the ritual (sacramental) action, not on a change of the elements. In the cup blessed and the bread we break, we have a communion in the body and blood of the Lord (1 Cor 10:16). We recognize the risen Jesus in the breaking of the bread (Luke 24:35). "Whoever eats my flesh and drinks my blood remains in me and I in him" (John 6:56). From the second century Christian theology has spoken of the bread and wine as the body and blood of Jesus. But as Henri de Lubac noted over fifty years ago, in the eleventh and twelfth centuries a shift took place in eucharistic theology. Prior to that theologians used the term "true body" of Christ *(verum corpus)* for the Church, and spoke of the Eucharist as the "mystical" body *(corpus mysticum).* But in the mid-eleventh century, in reaction to Berengarius' heretical eucharistic doctrine, *"mysticum"* in reference to the Eucharist was dropped, to be later applied to the Church, while *verum,* true, was applied to the Eucharist.[11]

Since then, piety has focused too much on what happens to the gifts, to the exclusion of the action of the assembly in which the gifts, blessed, broken, poured out, and shared, become the symbol *(sacramentum)* of the Lord's presence. Rather than stressing the fruitfulness of communion, the emphasis was placed on the power of consecration and the "miracle of transubstantiation," the change of the bread and wine into the body and blood of Christ. Vatican II sought to address this imbalance, speaking not

10. Roger Mahony, "Gather Faithfully Together: A Guide for Sunday Mass," *Origins* 27/15 (1997) 248.

11. Henri de Lubac, *Corpus Mysticum* (Paris: Aubier, 1949) 95–96; 116–21; see also Paul McPartlan, *The Eucharist Makes the Church: Henri de Lubac and John Zizioulas in Dialogue* (Edinburgh: T&T Clark, 1993) 76–77.

simply of "real presence," but of a manifold presence of Christ, in the ordained minister, elements, sacraments, word, and assembly (cf. SC 7).

Yet even today, some Catholics interpret the Church's theological language in overly literal, common sense terms. They speak of Christ's "physical" presence, a term the tradition has generally avoided. Others seem to
suggest that the deepest meaning of Eucharist is to be found in the adoration of the reserved species. But as Nathan Mitchell has said, "In the Eucharist Christ is present not as an 'object' to be admired but as a person (a
'subject') to be encountered."[12]

Thus we need to ask, have we so focused on the bread and wine that
we have turned Christ's presence into a "thing to be admired" rather than
an encounter in his body, the Church. Has the Catholic experience of the
Eucharist become excessively individualistic rather than ecclesial? Have
we become captive to a second-level philosophical language, based on
medieval concepts of matter and form? Are we ready to say with conviction, the Church makes the Eucharist and the Eucharist makes the Church?
For it is precisely in the ritual action, breaking the bread and sharing in
the cup, that the Church has a communion in the risen Christ and becomes
his body (1 Cor 10:16-17).

Conclusions

Of all the changes brought about by the Second Vatican Council, the
most dramatic for the majority of Catholics were the changes in the liturgy.
The Catholic experience of worship has changed, both theologically and
practically. Theologically, the old emphasis on the Mass as a propitiatory
sacrifice offered to God by the priest has given way to a sense for the
communal worship of the entire Church. Practically, a simplified ritual,
vernacular language, a greater emphasis on Scripture, congregational
singing, Communion under both species, a diversity of liturgical roles—
all this has helped make the meaning of the liturgy more accessible to people.

But if the liturgy has been declericalized, it has also been to a considerable extent desacralized, and contemporary Catholics remain divided
over liturgical questions. Some want more changes, greater lay involvement, including lay preaching. Others lament the loss of the sacred and a
sense for the most profound dimension of the eucharistic mystery. Some
want to roll back the changes in the years since the council, while a minority
wants to return to pre-conciliar usage.

---

12. Nathan Mitchell, "Who Is at the Table: Reclaiming the Real Presence," *Commonweal* 122 (27 January 1995) 12.

The liturgical divisions in the Catholic community are not insignificant. They need to be addressed, so that the Eucharist might truly be the Church's great sacrament of unity rather than a cause of division. If we have made considerable progress in our liturgical celebration, we may need to reflect more deeply on the way we celebrate and on the nature of the eucharistic mystery itself.

But the majority of Catholics have accepted the new liturgy. As Archbishop Weakland says, "They are, for the most part, content with the liturgical renewal of Vatican II. They do not want to lose what has been gained."[13]

13. Weakland, "Liturgy and Common Ground," 11.

7

A New Evangelization

Since the Second Vatican Council evangelization has assumed a new importance in the self-awareness of the Church. The council itself, in contrast to Vatican I, which used the term "gospel" only once, mentions the gospel 157 times, uses the word "evangelize" 18 times and "evangelization" 31 times.[1] If evangelization has traditionally been understood as preaching the gospel to those who have not yet heard it, the concept has undergone at least two significant developments in the years since the council, largely through the emphasis given to it in the works of Pope Paul VI and Pope John Paul II.

First, recent magisterial teaching has emphasized that there is a social as well as a personal dimension to evangelization. The 1971 document of the Third Synod of Bishops, entitled "Justice in the World," specifically linked evangelization with a commitment to social transformation: "Action on behalf of justice and participation in the transformation of the world fully appear to us as a constitutive dimension of the preaching of the Gospel, or, in other words, of the Church's mission for the redemption of the human race and its liberation from every oppressive situation" (no. 6).

In 1975 Paul VI issued his important apostolic exhortation *Evangelii nuntiandi,* in which he taught that not just individuals, but also cultures need to be evangelized (no. 20). Evangelization has a social dimension which involves human rights, family life, peace, justice, development,

1. Avery Dulles, "John Paul II and the New Evangelization," *America* 166 (1992) 53; see also his "John Paul and the New Evangelization—What Does It Mean?" in *John Paul II and the New Evangelization,* ed. Ralph Martin and Peter Williamson (San Francisco: Ignatius Press, 1995) 25–39.

and liberation (no. 29); Pope Paul argued that evangelization and liberation are linked because the person "who is to be evangelized is not an abstract being but is subject to social and economic questions." Thus he sees a profound connection between evangelization and social justice; the church's mission includes both evangelization and liberation. Yet the finality of evangelization remains specifically religious (no. 31).

Pope John Paul II quoted extensively from *Evangelii nuntiandi* in his address to the Latin American bishops at their meeting in Puebla in 1979, warning, as had his predecessor, against any reduction of the gospel to a secular ideology, but at the same time affirming the place of works on behalf of justice as part of the Church's evangelizing mission.

Second, Pope John Paul II has repeatedly called the Church to a "new evangelization," a term he used for the first time at Port-au-Prince, Haiti, on March 9, 1983. In later documents he has developed considerably this notion, particularly in his 1990 encyclical *Redemptoris missio*.[2] The encyclical speaks of a twofold end. First, a primary evangelization for those who have not yet heard the gospel, thus, the Church's traditional mission *ad gentes,* "to the nations." Second, a "new" evangelization or re-evangelization of those who have already heard Christ proclaimed, in other words, those large numbers of Christians who no longer consider themselves members of the Church (no. 30).

Much of Europe is now effectively post-Christian. As of 1995, regular Sunday observance for Catholics in Western Europe varied from 13 to 31 percent (13 percent in Belgium, 18 percent in Germany, 31 percent in Italy). Among the younger groups in France, 8 percent attend Mass on Sundays, a number that increases slightly for those above sixty. In the Netherlands only 24 percent of newborn babies are baptized. In 1998 30 percent of the population in the western part of Germany and 78 percent in the eastern part did not belong to any church. The statistics for Protestants are even lower.[3] In Eastern Europe and the former Soviet Union, where years of Communism have resulted in several generations without any Christian education, many have been neither baptized nor evangelized. In the old East Germany, two-thirds of the adults and 90 percent of the youth are unbaptized. We have already mentioned the losses in Latin America.

But the Pope is not talking merely of non-practicing Christians. There are vast areas in Asia, Africa, Latin America, and Oceania that have yet to be evangelized. He calls attention to new cultural groups, those living in inner cities, migrants, refugees, young people, and those heavily influ-

---

2. John Paul II, "Redemptoris missio," *Origins* 20/34 (1991) 541–68.
3. Cf. Jan Kerkhofs, "Europe needs therapy," *The Tablet* (July 24, 1999) 1015–16.

enced by the mass media. For John Paul, "The proclamation of Christ and the kingdom of God must become the means for restoring the human dignity of these people." Finally, evangelization must be directed at modern culture itself, the "new culture" created by modern means of communication as well as other forms of the "Areopagus" (cf. Acts 17:22-31) in the modern world such as scientific research and international relations (no. 37).

The Pope's understanding of the new evangelization is itself "evangelical" in a sense that many evangelical Protestants would appreciate. He stresses that the "kingdom of God is not a concept, a doctrine or a program subject to free interpretation, but is before all else a person with the face and name of Jesus of Nazareth" (no. 18). What lies at the center of the church's mission and life is the proclamation of the mystery of the love of God who invites us into a personal relationship with him in Christ. This is the good news which changes both individuals and human history (no. 44). This "missionary activity" or "work of evangelization" is the responsibility of the whole church—"for all Christians, for all dioceses and parishes, church institutions and associations." It "is the primary service which the church can render to every individual and to all humanity in the modern world" (no. 2).

In his 1999 apostolic exhortation "Ecclesia in America," delivered in the course of a pastoral visit to Mexico, John Paul returned even more explicitly to evangelization as a "fresh encounter with Jesus Christ" (no. 7).[4] Quoting from the 1997 Special Synod on the Americas, the Pope speaks of three places where Christ can be encountered. First, in the "sacred Scripture read in the light of tradition, the fathers and the magisterium, and more deeply understood through meditation and prayer." Second, in the liturgy. And third, in "the persons, especially the poor, with whom Christ identifies himself" (no. 12).

Thus John Paul II has placed evangelization at the heart of the Church's mission. He relates it to the Church's social teaching in *Centesimus annus* (1991): "Teaching and spreading her social doctrine are part of the church's evangelizing mission" (no. 54).[5] Similarly, his efforts to bring about more cooperative relationships among the world religions as well as his reaffirmation of the Church's ecumenical efforts in his most recent encyclical *Ut unum sint*[6] are rooted in his vision of the Church's evangelical mission. In his 1996 visit to Germany, John Paul again emphasized that "evangelization and ecumenism are indissolubly linked" and he

4. John Paul II, "Ecclesia in America," *Origins* 28 (1999) 567.
5. John Paul II, "Centesimus Annus," *Origins* 21 (1991) 1–24.
6. John Paul II, "Ut unum sint," *Origins* 25 (1995) 49–72.

stressed that the "task of evangelization equally concerns all Christians—Catholic, Orthodox and Protestant.[7] Finally, he has stressed that interreligious dialogue is itself a form of evangelization, not to proselytize, but because it involves sharing with another our own experience of God and God's salvific activity in the Lord Jesus.

Finding the Language that Gives Life

History will remember Pope John Paul II for the important role he played in the collapse of Communism across Eastern Europe and for the great emphasis he has placed on the Church's evangelical mission. If we take that mission seriously, we need to address the question of the language with which we present the gospel. How do we find the language that gives life? Therefore, in this chapter I would like to consider critically various efforts to express the Good News of salvation in Christ in contemporary language and then outline some of the characteristics of a truly evangelical theology.

After more than twenty years of teaching theology to undergraduates in a Roman Catholic university, my own impression is that the traditional language in which we try to present the Good News doesn't have much meaning to many today, particularly to young adults, and that most of the efforts to re-express the gospel in a more contemporary idiom fail also.

One of the most difficult issues to come to terms with is the question of salvation and redemption: what do we mean precisely when we say that Jesus paid a price, died in our place, justified us, reconciled us to God and thus to one another? Are these traditional expressions of how Jesus saves us still able to communicate to educated Christians today?[8] Does the gospel strike us as "good news" that frees us and offers us new life?

Many people today feel no particular need to be saved or justified. Though many of the students I teach are not practicing their faith, they speak comfortably about a God who is kind and forgiving, a God who is "there" for them. One does not sense that a relationship with God has made any demands on them. They have no sense of a personal need for grace or forgiveness and rarely use the language of discipleship or conversion. Many are functional Pelagians. As one observed: "I'm able to live a good life on my own; I don't really need the Church." When I hear statements like this I become more sympathetic with what Peter Kreeft is trying to say when he writes that "well over three-quarters of all the 'edu-

7. John Paul II, "Linking Evangelization and Ecumenism," *Origins* 26 (1996) 140.
8. Cf. Roger Haight, "Jesus and Salvation: An Essay in Interpretation," *Theological Studies* 55 (1994) 225–51.

cated' Catholic college students I have taught do not know, after twelve years of catechism, how to get to heaven."[9]

Furthermore, in spite of the strong emphasis on "social justice" on many Catholic college campuses, it is not clear that Catholic students have really accepted or internalized the life of discipleship that is at the heart of Jesus' preaching of the kingdom. Martin Tripole, a Jesuit with many years' teaching experience at St. Joseph's University in Philadelphia, argues that Jesuit campuses have settled for social-service programs rather than the transformation of their students on the basis of gospel values: "We do not succeed in transforming the self-identity of our students, so that they define themselves as children of God, redeemed by the death and resurrection of Christ, committed to him personally and motivated by his values, so that they accept the spirit of the Beatitudes as the acceptable form of Christian and human living."[10]

The problem of translating the message of the gospel into a contemporary idiom is complicated by fact that our churches are divided by different understandings of precisely what God has done for us in Christ. Catholics and mainline Protestant churches generally stress the corporate nature of our salvation, with its ecclesial and social implications. Evangelical churches and more conservative Catholics emphasize an individualistic understanding of salvation based on Christ's substitutionary atonement. In Latin America these different approaches frequently bring the two traditions into conflict. In the United States there are conflicts between an integralism hostile to theological developments and change in the Church and an academic theology which too often has become secularized, overly specialized, and with little connection to the life of believers, as we saw earlier.[11]

So how do we find a theological language that gives life without losing the essential meaning of the gospel? I would like to briefly explore five theological languages that attempt to do this, examining each in terms of its key metaphors, themes, and priorities. We will consider the languages of evangelical individualism, ecclesiocentrism, liberation theology, spiritual therapy, and a pluralistic theocentrism.

---

9. Peter Kreeft, *Fundamentals of the Faith: Essays in Christian Apologetics* (San Francisco: Ignatius, 1988) 15.

10. Martin Tripole, *Faith Beyond Justice: Widening the Perspective* (St. Louis: Institute of Jesuit Sources, 1994) 135.

11. Randy L. Maddox explores the problem of the professionalization of academic theology in "The Recovery of Theology as a Practical Discipline," *Theological Studies* 51 (1990) 650–72.

Evangelical Individualism

The contemporary fundamentalist and evangelical movements have their roots deep within the revivalism that characterized eighteenth- and nineteenth-century Protestant Christianity in the United States and elsewhere. Specifically, the term "fundamentalism" is used to describe a conservative reaction to a Protestantism moving increasingly in a liberal direction in the period from 1870 to 1920. Thus, a basic characteristic is a militant hostility to liberal theology and to those values associated with "secular humanism," combined with a strong commitment to proclaiming salvation through a personal relationship with Jesus.

"Evangelicalism" is a broader term. It describes those who remain strongly committed to the older Protestant evangelical understanding of Christianity. George Marsden describes the essential of evangelical belief: (1) the Reformation doctrine of the final authority of the Bible, (2) the real historical character of God's saving work recorded in Scripture, (3) salvation based on the redemptive work of Christ, (4) the importance of evangelism and missions, and (5) the importance of a spiritually transformed life.[12]

Evangelicals can be found in most Protestant denominations. Though there are exceptions, their theological language tends to be individualistic rather than communal. The dominant metaphor is the "born again" conversion experience, a personal acceptance of Jesus Christ as one's personal Lord and Savior and the promise of everlasting life. This emphasis on a personal saving experience gives a strongly individualistic character to evangelical Christianity, while the belief that no one can be saved apart from explicit faith in Jesus grounds their evangelical zeal. Key theological themes include justification by faith alone, substitutionary atonement, the clarity and sufficiency of Scripture, inerrancy, supernaturalism, a strong personal morality, and the second coming of Christ.

Evangelicalism has often been accused of being anti-intellectual.[13] An evangelical approach to Scripture often results in a christology that fails to do justice to the humanity of Jesus and a biblicism which substitutes an infallibility of the text for the living tradition of the Church. At the same time, the individualistic strain in evangelical theology and the strong Calvinist influence makes ecclesiology relatively unimportant. In Avery Dulles' categories, they follow a "church as herald" ecclesiol-

12. George M. Marsden, *Understanding Fundamentalism and Evangelicalism*, 4–5; see also Mark A. Noll, *The Scandal of the Evangelical Mind* (Grand Rapids, Mich.: Eerdmans, 1994) 8.
13. See Noll, *The Scandal of the Evangelical Mind.*

ogy.[14] The true Church is the invisible assembly of the elect which cuts across denominational lines; their ecclesial life is generally non-liturgical and rarely concerned with ecumenism which is associated with the program of liberal Protestantism.

Evangelical Christianity emphasizes our promise of salvation and everlasting life through a personal relationship with Jesus. But its approach to Scripture, particularly its doctrine of inerrancy with its resulting literalism, inhibits considerably the possibility of dialogue with a postmodern, secular culture. While evangelicals are often generous in supporting relief agencies such as World Vision, their theology does not generally stress the social implications of the gospel. Since the kingdom of God is seen primarily as an eschatological reality, evangelical morality is much more personal than social. There are exceptions such as the "new evangelicals," for example, those belonging to Sojourners community in Washington, D.C. But evangelical moral concerns are more typically represented by groups such as the Moral Majority, the Christian Coalition, and James Dobson's "Focus on the Family," with their emphasis on personal morality and "family values."

Ecclesiocentrism

If evangelicals identify the salvation with a personal "born again" experience, conservative Catholicism makes it identical with incorporation into the Church; this becomes the primary purpose of evangelization. As Dulles has said, "The apologetically oriented theology of recent centuries . . . was too rationalistic and ecclesiocentric to be called evangelical. The primary goal of that theology was to argue unbelievers into Catholic faith and induce a docile acceptance of 'whatever the Church teaches.'"[15] The kingdom of God is too easily identified with the Church, understood on the basis of Dulles' institutional model. The dominant metaphor for Church is a hierarchically ordered society rather than the People of God or a communion *(koinonia)* of diverse members. Church membership is defined in terms of communion in doctrine, sacraments, and hierarchical government. This approach was too often typical of pre-Vatican II Catholicism.

One still finds these strong ecclesiocentrist tendencies in many of the movements and groups that make up the conservative Catholic subculture we considered in chapter one. Many of these Catholics are not open to the Church's social teaching or to ecumenism. They approach Protestantism,

---

14. Cf. Avery Dulles, *Models of the Church* (Garden City, N.Y.: Doubleday, 1974) 71–82.

15. Avery Dulles, "Evangelizing Theology," *First Things* 61 (March 1996) 28.

not by trying to find areas of agreement which might lead towards ecclesial reconciliation, as does official Catholic ecumenism, but by trying to show that the Reformation was illegitimate in the first place.

Liberation Theology

The emergence of liberation theology in Latin America has led to a new evangelical language that stresses liberation as the hermeneutic for understanding and proclaiming the gospel. Metaphors for liberation theology include the Exodus from Egypt, the Promised Land, and Jesus' symbol of the kingdom of God, particularly the Beatitudes and his Sermon on the Mount. From a liberationist perspective, salvation in Christ means liberation from sin, oppression, unjust social structures, and ultimately death. Among its key themes are discipleship, a spirituality of martyrdom, the importance of praxis, and, thus, the contextual nature of theology. Sin and morality are understood primarily in social rather than personal terms. Liberation christology emphasizes the historical Jesus and his identification with the poor and the marginalized. Its church-as-servant ecclesiology stresses the Church's prophetic, social/critical function and seeks to empower the poor through the creation of basic Christian communities.

The language of salvation as social liberation is strong in the Third World countries of Central and Latin America, Africa, and the Philippines and has led to new expressions of feminist, gay, and ethnic theologies in the United States. These liberation theologies have shown the importance of context and social location for theological reflection and have sought to give voice to those who have been voiceless.

But this contextual emphasis has also led to increasingly specialized theologies focusing on the interests of particular disadvantaged groups. Influenced by postmodernist criticism, these contextual theologies tend to regard all knowledge as politically constructed on the basis of power, gender, ethnicity, and social status. Many of them, driven by ideological concerns, have to a significant degree lost touch with the life of faith of the Christian community; they seem secular rather than evangelical or religious. One hears little about the person of Jesus himself as the Good News, the one who delivers us from sin and death.[16]

Spiritual Therapy

For many affluent, middle-class Christians, Christianity has been reduced to a substitute, psychological faith, a type of therapy. Philip Reiff

16. See for example, Thomas Weinandy, "Why Catholics Should Witness Verbally to the Gospel," *New Oxford Review* 60/6 (1993) 16–18.

describes the therapeutic as the "unreligion of the age" which provides "a manipulable sense of well-being."[17] According to Michael Downey, the therapeutic "has almost eclipsed the salvific as the governing category in spirituality."[18] From this perspective, salvation or new life in Christ is understood as a self-actualization and healing from personal tragedies, psychological wounds, dysfunctional families, addictive behavior, co-dependency, workaholism, and other forms of inauthentic existence. Spirituality means getting one's life together, reducing stress, or avoiding burnout, but little is said about a life of discipleship, participation in the paschal mystery of Jesus, or the social dimensions of the gospel.

The basic metaphor is Jesus as healer and friend, the tolerant Jesus who makes everything O.K., not the Jesus of the gospels who makes demands on us. Key themes include the resurrection, healing, unconditional acceptance, the priority of subjective experience, the importance of affectivity, intimacy, and sexuality, and a holistic spirituality. Its ecclesiological tendency is to see the Church as an ideal, healing community, and many move from one community or tradition to another until they find a comfortable fit. The desire for a psychological healing with spiritual overtones has contributed to the success of contemporary writers like Scott Peck, Thomas Moore, and Deepak Chopra.

Many looking for a spiritual dimension to their lives are indifferent, if not hostile, towards "institutional" religion. Wade Clark Roof has emphasized the highly subjective approach to religion of the "Baby Boomers" who "value experience over beliefs, distrust institutions and leaders, stress personal fulfillment yet yearn for community, and are fluid in their allegiances."[19] Tom Beaudoin has analyzed the popular culture which has shaped "Generation X," those young adults born between the early 1960s and the late 1970s. He finds this culture deeply suspicious of religious institutions but open to spirituality. It emphasizes the sacred nature of experience, finds a religious dimension to suffering, and accepts ambiguity as central to faith.[20]

Thus many today consider themselves spiritual, but not necessarily religious. Their personal faith is highly individualistic and subjective.

17. Philip Reiff, *The Triumph of the Therapeutic: Uses of Faith After Freud* (Chicago: University of Chicago Press, 1987) 13 (first published 1966).

18. Michael Downey, "Christian Spirituality: Changing Currents, Perspectives, Challenges," *America* 170/11 (1994) 10.

19. See for example, Wade Clark Roof, *A Generation of Seekers: the Spiritual Journey of the Baby Boomer Generation* (San Francisco: Harper/San Francisco, 1993).

20. Tom Beaudoin, *Virtual Faith: The Irreverent Spiritual Quest of Generation X* (San Francisco: Jossey-Bass, 1998) 41–42.

Doctrines, moral teachings, and church affiliations are accepted or rejected, not on the basis of external criteria such as their agreement with the biblical witness, the Christian tradition, or the apostolic Church, but rather because they agree or disagree with "my values" or "my experience." They seek "a God I am comfortable with," a "church that meets my needs," and "my personal spirituality." Truth is thus reduced to personal feeling. In his highly acclaimed *Habits of the Heart,* Robert Bellah profiles a woman, Sheila Larson, who calls her own personal religion "Sheilaism," named after herself.[21] She symbolizes many today who create their own religions which are non-confessional, indifferent to doctrine, and eclectic, combining elements of the Christian tradition with those from other faiths, New Age philosophy, parapsychology, and various self-help programs based on the twelve-step program of Alcoholics Anonymous.[22] Their privatized "spiritualities" are in some way analogous to the electronic church of the TV evangelists; salvation in your living room without real involvement in the Christian community.

Pluralistic Theocentrism

Finally, we should at least consider a contemporary theological language which seeks to reinterpret salvation in Christ, and thus, the Church's evangelical mission, in such a way as to make possible a fruitful dialogue with the great world religions. Heinz Schlette sees these religions as the ordinary way of salvation for their adherents.[23] Paul Knitter and John Hick argue that Christian theology should renounce its claim of superiority by moving beyond its doctrine that salvation is through Christ alone.[24] For Hans Küng, a religion which lowers the dignity of individuals, groups, or peoples is a false religion, while a true religion is one that serves this criterion.[25]

21. Robert N. Bellah, et al., *Habits of the Heart: Individualism and Commitment in American Life* (Berkeley: University of California Press, 1985) 221.

22. Cf. Meredith B. McGuire, "Mapping Contemporary American Spirituality," *Christian Spirituality Bulletin* 5/1 (1997) 4.

23. Heinz R. Schlette, *Towards a Theology of Religion* (New York: Herder and Herder, 1966) 102.

24. Paul F. Knitter, *No Other Name? A Critical Survey of Christian Attitudes Towards the World Religions* (Maryknoll, N.Y.: Orbis, 1985) 142; John Hick, "The Non-Absoluteness of Christianity," *The Myth of Christian Uniqueness,* ed. John Hick and Paul F. Knitter (Maryknoll, N.Y.: Orbis, 1987) 22–23.

25. Hans Küng, *Theology for the Third Millennium: An Ecumenical View* (New York: Doubleday, 1988) 244.

What these theologians are calling for is a shift from a christocentric to a theocentric Christian theology, one that recognizes that salvation can be mediated for non-Christians through the great world religions as well as through a commitment to transcendent values such as justice, peace, and concern for the poor and the powerless. Thus salvation is seen as deliverance from whatever alienates us from ourselves, others, and the divine life. From a christological perspective, Jesus reveals that a relationship with God requires a proper relationship to other human beings, one based on justice, love, and service. The Church proclaims God's presence by witnessing to these values; it is a servant Church.

Towards an Evangelical Theology

Each of these theological languages we have considered refracts important dimensions of the gospel, but each fails in significant ways, and so cannot provide the language that gives life. The challenge for the future is to develop a new evangelical theology, one that can harvest the best insights of the different theological languages we have been considering and still be truly evangelical. Here Catholics have much to learn from Evangelical Christians.

Richard Mouw has outlined three assumptions of contemporary evangelism. First, evangelism aims at conversion, with bringing a person into a personal relationship with God in Christ. Second, that conversion must be in some way experienced. Third, the experience of conversion includes the acceptance of some cognitive claims, an awareness of the "good news" of salvation in Christ.[26] Mouw's three assumptions about evangelism can provide a framework for our attempt here to outline an evangelical theology.

1. *An evangelical theology must first of all be christological.* This is not to suggest that the pneumatological is unimportant. It is. But at the same time, it is important to note that many contemporary theologies have come close to substituting an all-embracing pneumatology for christology. A *Christian* theology must be christocentric. Therefore, an evangelical theology must focus, not just on the social dimensions of Jesus' teaching, but on Jesus himself as the personal embodiment of God's salvation. The person of Jesus cannot be separated from his work. Evangelicals often speak of this as "the scandal of particularity." In the words of Donald Bloesch, that means "that God became man at one point in history, that God revealed himself among one particular people in history, the Jews,

---

26. Richard J. Mouw, "Evangelism: The Very Idea!" *Pro Ecclesia* 7/2 (1998) 176.

and that his revelation in this people and in this person is definitive and final."[27]

The perennial temptation of liberal theology is to give up this christological focus, thus reducing Christian faith to ethics. But this is to ignore the witness of Scripture. In spite of the fact that the historical Jesus spoke not about himself but about the reign of God, Christians from the beginning proclaimed Jesus. They saw the intrinsic connection between the man and his message; they grasped intuitively what God had done in his death and resurrection, and so the preacher became the preached.

Even before Paul, the early Christians proclaimed that "Christ died for our sins in accordance with the scriptures." Paul cites this early formula to the Corinthians (1 Cor 15:3). In his efforts to proclaim this to others, he reached into his own religious tradition, using various images to make this Good News concrete. In Christ, God has "justified" us, made us righteous (Rom 4:25; 5:16-18), "reconciling the world to himself," not counting our sins against us (2 Cor 5:19). Jesus has brought about our reconciliation with God through his death (Rom 5:10). He has accomplished our "redemption" (1 Cor 1:30), paid the price for our sins with his blood (Rom 3:23-25). Even though we can acknowledge the metaphorical character of these expressions, that does not mean we can move beyond their christocentric focus.

Most of all, Paul saw that Jesus' victory over sin and death means that the power of death itself has been destroyed (Rom 8) and that those who believe in him will share in his resurrection. Belief in the resurrection is not negotiable. Jesus is the "first fruits" of the resurrection from the dead (1 Cor 15:23). An evangelical theology today must continue this emphasis on what God has done in Jesus; if it is not radically christocentric is not an evangelical theology.

2. An evangelical theology should also be ecclesiological. It should be able to combine a strong evangelical sense for a personal relationship with Jesus with a Catholic appreciation for the ecclesial nature of Christian faith, with its social, communal, and sacramental dimensions. For Catholics, new life in Christ is inseparable from life in the Church. The Church is the community of disciples of Jesus, united by baptism in one Spirit (1 Cor 12:13) and constituted as the body of Christ in the world through their communion *(koinonia)* in his body and blood (1 Cor 1:16-17). The Church mediates new life in Christ through its proclamation

---

27. Donald G. Bloesch, *Jesus Christ: Savior and Lord* (Downers Grove, Ill.: Inter-Varsity Press, 1997) 236.

(kerygma) and teaching *(didache),* its liturgical worship *(liturgia),* its ministry *(diakonia),* and its community *(koinonia).*

However, Catholics recognize the possibility of salvation "outside the Church." Here they differ from most Evangelical Christians who deny the possibility of salvation apart from explicit faith in Christ. In effect, this is to restrict the offer of saving grace to the preached word.

The axiom "no salvation outside the Church" *(extra ecclesiam nulla salus)* has a long history.[28] It was used by Church Fathers even before Augustine in reference to Christians who had separated themselves from the Church. But Augustine's emphasis on the necessity of baptism and his pessimistic view of human nature in light of his teaching on original sin resulted in an intensification of the position; he specifically rejected the possibility of salvation for Jews and pagans, whether they had heard the gospel or not, and he taught that even unbaptized infants were damned. The axiom became the official teaching of the Church. As late as 1863 Pope Pius IX proclaimed: "It is a well-known Catholic dogma that no one can be saved outside the Catholic Church" (DS 2867).

But Pius IX also acknowledged that some who remained outside the Church because of "invincible ignorance" might be saved if they cooperated with divine grace. In doing this, he gave recognition to another tradition which had been developing in the Church since the "discovery" of the new world at the end of the fifteenth century. Catholics formed on the *Baltimore Catechism* knew that an upbaptized person who "loves God above all things and desires to do all that is necessary for his salvation" could receive "baptism of desire,"[29] a rather devious way of including them in the Church. Finally, the Second Vatican Council made the possibility of salvation outside the Church a matter of official church teaching. The council taught that those who sincerely seek God and, helped by grace, strive to do God's will, can attain to everlasting salvation (LG 16).

But this development in Catholic doctrine in no way lessens the urgency of the Church's evangelical mission. First, the doctrine of original sin describes a real, existential reality. For sinful men and women, living in a world itself damaged by sin, responding to grace is not an easy matter. The power of sin to "harden" our hearts should not be underestimated. We need the grace of Christ, God's self-revelation, the one who is himself the way, the truth, and the life (John 14:6).

---

28. See Francis A. Sullivan, *Salvation Outside the Church? Tracing the History of the Catholic Response* (New York: Paulist, 1992).

29. *A Catechism of Christian Doctrine,* rev. ed., Baltimore Catechism (Paterson, N.J.: St. Anthony Guild, 1948) 263.

Second, while evangelicals tend to emphasize an individualistic, forensic understanding of justification, Catholics see justifying grace as transformative. Grace effects both individuals and their relationships with one another. Grace perfects nature; those who have been justified enjoy a new life in the Spirit. Neither Paul's sacramental realism nor the Johannine theology of the divine indwelling can be neglected. From this perspective, the Church becomes all the more important. For it is the Church, the body of Christ, which makes visible the risen Christ's presence in history, mediating his new life to others. Thus the Church can be "a kind of sacrament of intimate union with God, and of the unity of all [human] kind" (LG 1).

3. *An evangelical theology must be rooted in the historic Christian tradition.* Christianity stands or falls with the affirmation that God's self-revelation takes place in history in the person of Jesus. The New Testament witnesses to that revelation. It is handed on in the Church and develops as the Church struggles to better express the faith it proclaims in doctrinal and credal formulations. In this way the tradition, expressed in the Church's Scripture, creeds, and doctrine, safeguards the "good news" of salvation in Christ.

Thus the "good news" of salvation in Christ involves a doctrinal content. Christian faith cannot be reduced to a general openness to God, let alone to the demand for moral living. Nor does theological reflection need to begin anew in each generation. Its necessary task of finding a more adequate expression of the faith fails if it simply surrenders the received doctrine of the Church to the latest theories of the few in the academy. Here the magisterium has an important role to play.

4. *An evangelical theology should emphasize an integral conversion of life.* Life in the Spirit means more than simply claiming a relationship with Jesus; it affects the whole person. This means that a genuine conversion should affect the various levels or patterns of our experience—affective, intellectual, moral as well as religious. It means moving beyond the prejudices and grudges that narrow and cramp our affective lives. An evangelical theology should be able to show how the grace of the Spirit brings about healing and wholeness in our personal lives without reducing it to a special interest theology or to a spiritual therapy or self-help program.

A genuine conversion must be both personal and social. A genuinely Christian morality addresses both aspects of our lives; it cannot be reduced to a middle-class emphasis on "family values" or restricted to questions dealing with sexual conduct. As Johann Baptist Metz has written,

Christianity in its essence is a messianic practice of discipleship; yet too often it has become no more than a "bourgeois religion."[30] Therefore, an evangelical theology should be able to incorporate the liberating, critical power of the gospel, reclaimed for the Church by recent magisterial social teachings and the theologies of liberation, as well as a concern for personal morality.

Finally, an integral conversion also affects our intellectual life. It means a willingness to admit evidence that runs counter to our cherished ideas and challenges our worldviews. It means the willingness to move beyond fundamentalist approaches to faith which refuse to acknowledge the compatibility of faith and reason. In short, it means a willingness to change one's mind.

Thus an evangelical theology should be able to combine a concern for bringing people to new life in Christ with a theological reflection that is intellectually respectable. It should be able to give expression to the mystery of salvation in a way that speaks to those living in a secular, postmodern culture. It should affirm the normativity of the biblical tradition as well as the living tradition of the Church precisely as a tradition which is able to raise new questions and arrive at deeper theological understandings of its faith. It should affirm the teaching authority of the Church without lapsing into a magisterial fundamentalism.

Conclusions

The Catholic Church has continued its missionary efforts through its religious orders and a growing number of lay associate programs. But the Church has not been very effective at reaching out to the many who have left its ranks. Catholics still make up 25 percent of the American population, just as they did at the beginning of the century. But with the millions of Hispanic immigrants in the last twenty years, that number should be considerably higher.

The success of RCIA programs around the country is evidence that local Catholic communities continue to draw converts to the Church. But the numbers in those programs are small in proportion to the enormous number of the "unchurched" today. And unfortunately, it is too often true that the majority of Catholics have left the task of sharing their faith with their postmodern neighbors to their evangelical brothers and sisters.

Pope John Paul II in particular will be remembered for reminding the Church of its evangelical mission in a secularized world. But few

30. Johann Baptist Metz, *The Emergent Church: The Future of Christianity in a Postbourgeois World* (New York: Crossroad, 1986) 27.

theologians in North America or Western Europe have shown much interest in evangelization. Avery Dulles has written on the need to make Catholic theology more evangelical.[31] Scott Hahn is attempting to develop a theology that is both evangelical and Catholic. And others are aware of the need for an evangelical theology able speak to all people, those who come from Christian backgrounds and cultures and those who have not yet heard the gospel, the poor and the uneducated, as well as modern men and women.[32]

But the Church has not been very successful in developing a language that is both evangelical and at the same time intellectually respectable. It cannot settle for a new theory of double truth, erecting a new divide between faith and reason. Nor can it enter into the dialogue with other faiths and cultures which will be so important in the next millennium if it remains bound to a biblical fundamentalism. The Spirit of God is not limited by the structures of the Church, as conservative Catholics sometimes seem to hold, or confined to the medium of the proclaimed word, as many evangelicals believe. Like the wind, the Spirit blows where it wills (cf. John 3:8).

Contemporary theology makes every effort to dialogue with culture, using its philosophical and academic modes of discourse. But it too often has become separated from the life of the Church and the faith of ordinary believers; it is not clear at all to many today that it is able or even interested in leading others to that personal and profound meeting with the Savior which must always be at the heart of Christian proclamation. Its interests too often seem academic or ideological rather than evangelical, and too many theologians in the academy take the position that the faith development of their students is not really their responsibility. If so many young Catholics are ignorant of the gospel tradition, these theologians must share the blame with parents and Church.

A truly evangelical theology must always be christological, ecclesiological, rooted in the historic Christian tradition, and emphasize an integral conversion of life. If theologians could develop such a theology, they would do the Church a great service.

---

31. Avery Dulles, "Evangelizing Theology," *First Things* 61 (1996) 27–32.

32. Cf. Allan Figueroa Deck, "Latino Religion and the Struggle for Justice: Evangelization as Conversion," *Journal of Hispanic/Latino Theology* 4/3 (1997) 28–41.

Towards Common Ground in Theology

In spite of the divisions in the Catholic community today, the Church is still very much alive and healthy. The real life of the Church is evident in its local communities, its parishes. As Charles Morris says at the end of his fine book *American Catholic,* "the people in the parishes are, in the main, more sensible than extremists in the professorate. They are not radical feminists, cultic 'earth-goddess' worshipers, Marxist poststructuralists, or feckless hedonists who seek an end to all rules."[1] But neither are they convinced that the ancient structure of the Catholic Church will collapse if Catholics use a more inclusive language in their prayer, stand during the Eucharistic Prayer, welcome and support their gay and lesbian children, or disagree with the pope over birth control or the ordination of women.

According to Andrew Greeley, the polarization is "among the elite who are screaming at each other and to whom most Catholics are paying no attention."[2] Archbishop Rembert Weakland's characterization of the largest group in his archdiocese is insightful. He describes them as holding the middle ground. They are proud of the present pope but don't read what he writes. Nor do they read the publications of the Catholic right or the left. Their primary concern is for vital parishes, with good liturgies and preaching, effective educational programs, and an ability to introduce their children to the riches of the faith. They like their priests, but expect them to be able to work with others. They are pragmatic; they try to accept the prohibition of the ordination of women—"at least for now"—but

1. Charles R. Morris, *American Catholic* (New York: Random House, 1997) 430.
2. Andrew Greeley, "Polarized Catholics? Don't Believe Your Mail!" *America* 176/6 (1997) 14.

cannot understand why the Church cannot ordain married men to meet the obvious need for more priests. They take a common-sense approach to questions of sexuality. They are not against rules or boundaries, but want the Church to be more flexible, as they must be in raising their children. They do not want a Church that says no to everything modern. Weakland finds these same attitudes across the sociological spectrum, from working poor to middle-class suburbanites.[3]

Still, the divisions in the Church today are serious. Many on the right advocate an uncompromising adherence to what they understand as the received tradition. They try to maintain in the face of contrary evidence that church teaching does not change, that what is needed is not dialogue but clear and authoritative teaching, that all the answers to contemporary questions can be found in the new *Catechism of the Catholic Church*, that those who don't agree should leave the Church. But such an approach is neither wise nor Catholic. Others on the left seem to think that welcoming the changes they advocate would immediately give the Church new life and vitality, heedless of the growing anxiety on the right and the threat of further fragmentation.

How can the Catholic Church remain a community united in faith and mission? There is much that Catholics can learn from similar divisions in the mainline Protestant churches. In his book *Claiming the Center,* Jack Rogers observes that the Presbyterian Church in the United States has been dominated by conflict between the 15 percent on the ideological right and the 10 percent on the ideological left, leaving the center too often leaderless and inarticulate.[4] He says that since the 1960s the Church has done three things:

> First, it has emphasized the exceptions rather than the rules and thus has conceded leadership in forming the values of society to more conservative bodies. Second, it has stressed alternative methods of Christian living and thus given the appearance of negating and rejecting traditional religious and family values. Third, it has made its treatment of all issues so complex and tentative that most people have turned elsewhere for positive guidance.[5]

Rogers' argument is that the Presbyterian Church needs to reclaim the center. Cardinal Bernardin termed this effort to find unity in diversity a

---

3. Rembert G. Weakland, "Reflections for Rome," *America* 178/13 (1998) 12–13.

4. Jack Rogers, *Claiming the Center: Churches and Conflicting Worldviews* (Louisville: Westminster John Knox Press, 1995) xv.

5. Ibid., 175.

search for common ground. In this final chapter I would like to suggest some principles for finding "common ground" in theology. What is needed is a theology that is at once critical and yet faithful to the Catholic tradition.

Principles

1. *Catholic Inclusivity.* Catholicism by its very nature is inclusive. Its impulse is to join rather than to separate. The adjective "catholic," from the Greek *kath' holou,* means "referring to the whole," "total," or "universal." It was first applied to the Church, in the sense of the whole or universal Church, by Ignatius of Antioch about A.D. 110. As early as the third and fourth centuries the word "catholic" was being used to distinguish the great or true Church from groups or movements separate from it. Interestingly, those who separated themselves were called "heretics," from the Greek word *hairein,* meaning "to take" or "to choose," in the sense of taking a part rather than the whole. In other words, heresy means being sectarian rather than catholic.

2. *Legitimate Diversity.* The opposite of sectarianism is a concern for unity, for holding diversity and unity together in one communion. An old cliché has it that when a Protestant Christian comes up with a new understanding of the Gospel or a new insight into the Christian life, he or she establishes another church, whereas a Catholic in the same position founds a religious order, a community within the Church which gives expression to a special charism for Christian life or service. Yes, a cliché, but like all clichés, an expression which embodies a certain truth.

The important point is that Catholicism is open to all truth, and to diverse expressions of the truth. It is not the product of a single reformer or historical movement in post-New Testament Christian history. It does not find its identity in a single doctrine, like Lutheranism, with its emphasis on justification by faith alone. Unlike Reformed or Calvinist Christianity, it is not based on a single theological tradition. It is not defined by a single liturgical tradition, as is Anglicanism, which finds its principle of unity in the *Book of Common Prayer.* Nor is it committed to a single method of biblical interpretation, like evangelical and fundamentalist Protestantism, bound to a confessional notion of biblical inerrancy. To be Catholic is to be open to truth in all its expressions, to whatever is genuinely human or naturally good.

Thus Catholicism includes within itself a wide variety of theologies, spiritualities, and expressions of Christian life. It is pluralistic in its approach to the truth. Where the Reformation followed an "either/or" approach, Catholicism prefers to say "both/and." Not Scripture alone, but

Scripture and tradition; not grace alone, but grace and nature; not faith alone, but faith and works.

3. *Theological Humility.* In his later years, Karl Rahner spoke increasingly about the "incomprehensibility" of God.[6] Even though God has revealed himself in the person of Jesus and so we can attain to real knowledge about God, God is still the ultimate, transcendent mystery and remains beyond the ability of our minds to comprehend. Revelation in a real sense "unveils" the mystery, but it cannot dissolve it or take it away. The human response before this mystery is prayer, adoration, and surrender.

Our images, concepts, and words about God are all drawn from our experience, mediated by the biblical texts, the teachings of the Church, the experience of the mystics; thus they are culturally conditioned, human constructs. Our theological language, even if it enables us to go beyond the metaphorical, is at best analogical. A metaphor draws a comparison between two things which are ontologically unlike each other. Analogy recognizes a similarity in difference; it affirms something that is true of two things by reference to a prime analogue or focal point of meaning.[7] Our theological language is important. But it is always a "second order" language. It remains limited, removed by one or more levels of abstraction from the realities human and divine it seeks to describe. As Elizabeth Johnson says, "Whether expressed by metaphorical, symbolic, or analogical theology, there is basic agreement that the mystery of God is fundamentally unlike anything else we know of, and so is beyond the grasp of all our naming."[8]

Given the limited nature of our theological language, we need a certain theological humility. Particularly in a time of transition and change, it is important to realize that we do not have all the answers. There are many things we simply do not know, and new questions that we are not yet able to answer. Nor can every question can be answered by citing the *Catechism of the Catholic Church* or the *National Catholic Reporter.* The *NCR* is good for what's going on in the contemporary Church, but it is not the font of all wisdom. The new *Catechism* is a wonderful compendium of Catholic doctrine, but it does not reflect modern scholarship or address many contemporary concerns. Pope John Paul II speaks of it in his intro-

---

6. Karl Rahner, "Thomas Aquinas on the Incomprehensibility of God," *Journal of Religion* (Supplement) 58 (1978) 107–25.

7. Cf. David Tracy, *The Analogical Imagination: Christian Theology and the Culture of Pluralism* (New York: Crossroad, 1986) 408–13.

8. Elizabeth A. Johnson, *She Who Is: The Mystery of God in Feminist Discourse* (New York: Crossroad, 1992) 117.

duction as a "reference text" for catechisms prepared in various regions. It is not intended to provide answers for new questions.

The Church today is confronted by many difficult questions which need honest discussion, among them, the shortage of priests and the right of communities to the Eucharist, a more collegial style of church leadership, allowing the laity some participation in its decision-making processes and the formulation of its teaching, addressing the special concerns of women, minorities, the divorced, and those in mixed marriages, renewing its ethical teaching particularly in the area of sexuality, and allowing for greater adaptation and inculturation at local levels and in different cultures. These are challenges as great as any in the Church's history, and they arise, not out of a modern secular spirit, but precisely out of those currents of renewal unleashed by the Second Vatican Council. To address them we need to return to the biblical, liturgical, and patristic sources of our tradition as well as to take account of what we've learned from the social sciences and from other churches. We need to remember that truth is always greater than ourselves, that it encompasses more than our own concerns at any particular moment. We need not just to talk but to listen to each other; we need prayer, discernment, and the freedom to be led by the Spirit.

4. *Faith Seeking Understanding.* Christian theology is always a reflection on faith; as Pope John Paul II has written, the "very heart of theological inquiry will . . . be the contemplation of the mystery of the triune God."[9] Therefore it must be done by a believer, someone who is involved in the life and worship of the Christian community. Catholicism in particular is a sacramental faith; though theology is important, the Catholic experience of God in Christ is transmitted primarily through sacramental symbols and biblical narratives which speak not just to the intellect but also to the heart. Thus there is a genuine religious knowledge which comes from participation in the life of the community.

Furthermore, that community is catholic; it embraces the Christian community in its diversity of peoples, differences in social status, and viewpoints. To reduce the community to a conventicle of the *cognoscenti* or to a narrow sectarian orthodoxy, to a woman Eucharist or Tridentine Mass group, is to risk one's communion with the Catholic Church.

5. *Complementarity of Faith and Reason.* Catholicism must continue to acknowledge the complementarity of faith and reason, or as it might be expressed today, theology and science. Science and theology are different ways of knowing; they have different methodologies and different

---

9. John Paul II, "Fides et Ratio," *Origins* 28 (1998) 317–47, no. 93.

understandings of what counts as evidence. Yet both are ways of arriving at truth which is fundamentally one. It is impossible that what is true from the perspective of science would be contradicted by theology. Science and theology cannot be fundamentally in contradiction with one another. But that is not to say that what is theologically true can be "proved" by scientific investigation.

There has been ignorance and arrogance on both sides. Too many scientists have tried to reduce all knowledge to what can be known by the scientific method. Too many representatives of religion have ignored overwhelming scientific evidence to maintain positions determined by literalist or inerrantist understandings of Scripture. The infamous 1925 conviction of John Scopes for teaching evolution in a Tennessee school is just one sad example.

What is to be rejected is any separationism or "double truth" theory which would confine the truths of science and theology to entirely separate spheres. It is thus important to distinguish their respective fields of competence, the areas in which they overlap, as well as the kinds of affirmations that lie beyond them. The theory of evolution and the biblical doctrine of creation are not in contradiction to each other. One affirms that the world is the work of a creative deity; the other is a scientific explanation of how the world and its wonderful varieties of life developed.

Pope John Paul's 1998 encyclical *Fides et ratio* is timely in its appearance.[10] Faith and reason too often are at odds today, while philosophical reason itself has been marginalized (no. 47). It is not reason's role to pass judgment on the contents of faith, to determine what faith can affirm about the mystery of our salvation.

But neither should an appeal to faith require an attempt to integrate faith and reason on the basis of the categories of common sense or a biblical literalism, or giving up any effort at integration, to adopt a position of double truth. Faith adheres to God's self-revelation in the life, death, and resurrection of Jesus, witnessed by Scripture and the living tradition of the Church. That faith must always be expressed in a theological language that is both faithful to Scripture and the tradition and at the same time in harmony with the truths of scientific and philosophical reason. John Paul underlines this difference between faith and the language in which it is expressed; he says that "fundamental theology should demonstrate the profound compatibility that exists between faith and its need to find expression by way of human reason fully free to give its assent" (no. 67).

10. John Paul II, "Fides et Ratio," *Origins* 28 (1998) 317–47.

6. *Historical Consciousness.* The Church's eventual acceptance of modern biblical criticism and the return to the sources of Christian doctrine in Scripture, the liturgy, and the Fathers of the Church led to a theology which placed an enormous importance on historical investigation. Indeed Christian faith itself is historically mediated. It does not continually begin anew from some personal interpretation of Scripture, which leads only to a multiplicity of churches and sects. Rather, it has its origins in the story of Israel, its full expression in the person and history of Jesus of Nazareth, and is handed on through the Scriptures of both testaments, the tradition and life of the Church, its apostolic ministry, and its magisterium. At the same time, Christian truth in its entirety was not delivered to the Church by Christ and the apostles, neatly formulated in propositions. The implications of God's revelation in Christ continue to unfold as the Church ponders and reflects upon the mystery from which it lives. Thus there is a necessary development of doctrine which takes place over the centuries.

Historical consciousness stresses the concrete and particular; it presumes development and change based on new insights, the reinterpretation of traditional positions, and the incorporation of higher viewpoints. Its approach is inductive, not deducing conclusions from some concept of a universal nature, but synthesizing the results of empirical observation, critical, historical evidence, and personal experience. It recognizes that meaning emerges out of a historical process of investigation, that it develops, sometimes becomes frozen, and can change, but is always capable of reinterpretation and arriving at deeper insight.

The Catholic Church at the beginning of the twenty-first century presupposes this historical way of thinking for theological scholarship. Modern biblical and theological studies require careful investigation, research, and reformulation. The Congregation for the Doctrine of the Faith emphasized in its instruction *Mysterium Ecclesiae* (1973) that every "expression of revelation," whether Scripture, creed, dogmas, doctrine, or the teaching of the magisterium, is historically conditioned and therefore limited. Such limitations might come from the expressive power of the language or limited knowledge at the time, by the specific concerns that motivated the definition or statement, or by the "changeable conceptualities" or thought categories used.[11] For example, the monarchical concept of the Church which found its ultimate expression in the definition of papal primacy at the First Vatican Council in 1870 needs to be rethought

11. "Declaration in Defense of the Catholic Doctrine on the Church Against Certain Errors of the Present Day," *Origins* 3 (1973) 97–100.

and reformulated in the light of Vatican II's collegial understanding of church office. The 1993 document of the Pontifical Biblical Commission (PBC), "The Interpretation of the Bible in the Church,"[12] reaffirmed the necessity of historical-critical study of Scripture, giving it a kind of primacy over other methods of interpretation, and warning against the dangers of fundamentalism, as we saw earlier. Thus there is no excuse for an unhistorical approach to biblical scholarship or theology.

At the same time, the PBC warned against reducing biblical scholarship to a purely historical investigation of texts. Luke Timothy Johnson argues that such "hegemony of the historical critical method" has resulted in "the academic captivity of the church."[13] The PBC calls for a "rereading" or "actualization" of the Bible in the context of the Church's life, circumstances, and worship.

One does not need a German doctorate to read the Bible; Christians should read, study, and ponder the Scriptures daily. But if one is going to use Scripture in constructive theology or in apologetics, then it should be interpreted according to sound principles of biblical scholarship. The primary task of the exegete is to determine the meaning of the text in its proper literary and historical context, what is often referred to as the literal sense or historical meaning of the text.

The same concern for historical accuracy applies to the task of theology. Michael Novak used the term "non-historical orthodoxy" for the approach which identifies as doctrine teachings which have no real biblical or historical foundation.[14] An example would be the first draft of *Dei Verbum* which spoke of the "two sources" of revelation.

7. *An Ecclesial Theology.* Christian theology comes from and is at the service of the Christian community, the Church. This is particularly true for Catholic theology. Faith is mediated by the believing community; it is proclaimed, lived out, celebrated, expressed in various forms, and handed on to future generations through the Church. Thus there is a communal, ecclesial dimension of theology from the beginning. To the extent that the theologian becomes cut off from this community of faith, he or she is cut off from life in Christ. Once this happens to the theologian, theology becomes desiccated and withers. No longer reflection on a faith enlivened

12. *Origins* 23 (1994) 497–524.
13. Luke Timothy Johnson, *The Real Jesus: The Misguided Quest for the Historical Jesus and the Truth of the Traditional Gospels* (San Francisco: HarperSanFrancisco, 1996) 169.
14. Michael Novak, *The Open Church* (New York: Macmillan, 1964) especially chapter 5.

by the Spirit, it becomes merely an academic exercise, at best religious studies or the history of religions, but not theology.

The magisterium has a special role to play within the Church; its authority and unique role need to be acknowledged. Only the magisterium can say what is the faith of the Church and what is only theological opinion. It remains one of the Catholic Church's greatest strengths, allowing it to authoritatively reinterpret its tradition in the light of new questions. A theologian allergic to the Church's teaching authority, who did not respect the magisterium, recognizing its competence and honoring its important role, would not be "Catholic."

But the magisterium does not function independently of the Church; it is not a self-sufficient source. It is not over the Church but speaks for it. It must articulate what the Church believes. The old distinction between the "teaching Church" and the "learning Church" is inadequate; it presents a false division. Some Catholics continue to imagine the Church as an institution in which all authority comes from the pope down; disputed questions are answered simply by ascertaining what the pope or the pope and bishops have said.

In reality, the process is much more complicated. The Holy Spirit is active in the whole Church, not just in the hierarchy. The doctrine of the *sensus fidelium* and the ecclesial practice of reception indicate that there is a mutuality or interdependence between faithful and hierarchy. Critical reception of the teaching of the ordinary magisterium sometimes leads to reinterpretation, and on occasion, change. A number of examples of doctrinal development of this kind are evident in the decrees of the Second Vatican Council. The development of doctrine is always a complex process that involves the sense of the faithful, the critical work of theologians, various prophetic voices, and the authoritative teaching of the Church's bishops united with the pope.

8. *An Evangelical Theology.* If theology is a reflection on the good news of salvation revealed in Christ, then it must be an evangelical theology, concerned with sharing that Good News. Pope John Paul II has called the Church to a new consciousness of its evangelical mission. In *Redemptoris missio,* his encyclical on evangelization and mission, he warns about a "gradual secularization of salvation" which reduces Christianity to a merely human wisdom and humanity to its horizontal dimension (no. 11). Instead, the Church's proclamation is to introduce men and women "into the mystery of the love of God" who calls them "to enter into a personal relationship with himself in Christ" (no. 44).

A theology at the service of the Church must share this evangelical impulse. It cannot be a merely academic exercise, addressing social problems, hermeneutical issues, and ideological agendas. Nor should it be reduced to an apologetic justification and defense of the historical claims of the Catholic Church, particularly as a pre-critical popular Catholicism often perceives them.

An evangelical theology calls others into a personal relationship with Jesus, new life in his Spirit, and solidarity with all people; it presupposes conversion of life and communion in the Church. It refuses any separation of faith from historic creed or spirituality from theology and rejects the western privatization of faith which makes witnessing to or sharing the good news impossible. While the Catholic theological tradition is distinctive from that of evangelical Protestantism in a number of significant ways, there is much that Catholics and Catholic theology can learn from their evangelical brothers and sisters.

9. *An Ecumenical Theology.* There should also be an ecumenical dimension to Catholic theology. The Second Vatican Council, in committing the Catholic Church to the ecumenical movement, stressed that theology should be presented from an ecumenical point of view (UR 10). If a theology is to be truly "catholic," it must be concerned with truth in all its expressions, including those to be found among other churches and Christian communities. It should present different points of view honestly. At the same time, a Catholic theologian has a particular obligation to honestly represent Catholic doctrine in its entirety: "Nothing is so foreign to the spirit of ecumenism as a false conciliatory approach which harms the purity of Catholic doctrine and obscures its assured genuine meaning" (UR 11).

10. *A Hierarchy of Truths.* While no doctrinal statement is insignificant, not all doctrines are of the same degree of importance. The council affirmed that there exists "an order or 'hierarchy' of truths, since they vary in their relationship to the foundation of Christian faith" (UR 11). Doctrinal differences between Christians may reflect more the development of different insights rather than Church-dividing differences over the fundamental nature of the faith. Thus the hierarchy of truths is of great significance in ecumenism.

11. *Respect for the Other.* In 1997 Bishop Donald Wuerl of Pittsburgh issued a pastoral letter to his diocese entitled, "Speaking the Truth in Love: Christian Discourse Within the Church." Linking mutual respect with the Church's fundamental evangelical mission, he asked, "Who would be drawn to a community whose discourse is filled with rancor, mistrust and ha-

tred? We cannot highlight evangelization and then destroy its fondest hopes by the way we talk with or about one another."[15]

If we are to find "common ground" in our theology as well as in our Church, we need to learn how to talk with each other with greater respect. Cardinal Roger Mahony has observed that we are much better at dialogue with others than we are between and among ourselves, and he reminds us that dialogue does not always lead to agreement. "It has great value nonetheless in clarifying disagreements, which can then be faced and embraced with charity, respect, humility and love for the truth. And in the process, each one may be changed personally by virtue of the gifts exchanged."[16]

Conclusions

How can we learn to speak the truth as we see it in love rather than in rancor? We cannot do so without the willingness to presume good will on the part of the other, without respecting our dialogue partner, without the willingness to be converted ourselves. The Church needs more listening on all sides, liberals and conservatives, theologians and their critics, laity and members of the hierarchy, bishops and Rome. We've got to find a way to turn down the volume and—without abandoning our sense of what is truly important—step beyond our personal certainties and absolutist positions. We need to find ways to acknowledge our own failings and reach out to those who see things differently, so that we might rediscover the good in one another and the truth in positions different from our own.

Conservatives cannot hope to answer questions facing the Church today with simplistic appeals to authority or to the Church of the nineteenth century. They need to acknowledge more readily the historical nature of Christian faith, that doctrines develop, are reinterpreted, and sometimes change. They need to show a much greater concern for historical context in dealing with biblical or theological questions today.

Those on the left need to acknowledge more honestly the destructive nature of so many of their criticisms, as well as the anticlericalism that is often concealed in them. To speak of an egalitarian Church, a lay Church without a principle of order, is contrary to the Catholic tradition. It is also sociologically naïve. It has been tried before in Christian history, and has always failed. They may also have to ask if their relentless critique is really for the good of the Church.

15. Donald Wuerl, "Christian Discourse Within the Church," *Origins* 27 (1997) 290.

16. Roger Mahony, "Dialogue in the Church," *Origins* 28 (1998) 500.

Those on both sides need to find ways to address the theological illiteracy and ignorance of the tradition that afflicts so many young Catholics without having recourse to a non-historical orthodoxy or a magisterial fundamentalism. Catholic students need good, critical theology as well as courses in the riches of the Catholic tradition. Those who teach in colleges and universities should ask themselves if they are handing on that tradition or just the theories of the academy. If they have no concern for the religious lives of their students and their involvement in the community of faith, they are not doing a theology at the service of the Church. Catholic students deserve better.

The Church needs episcopal leaders willing to address real issues. Too often an exaggerated sense of loyalty to the pope prevents the bishops from raising the difficult questions they know that they face. But when this happens, they are failing not just the pope, but themselves as pastors who with the pope constitute the Church's highest authority and its teaching magisterium.

Finally, as William Shea of St. Louis University has written, Catholics need to pay more attention to the Protestant fundamentalist critique of Catholic belief and practice, including the charge made by so many Catholic converts to fundamentalist churches that they "never heard the gospel" in a Catholic church.[17] That charge may sometimes be true. If we continue to reduce our faith to an agenda of issues, whether of the right or the left, we won't have much to offer those who should be the Catholics of the next generation. Worse, we will have missed the chance to bring them and so many others into that personal and profound meeting with the Savior called for by Pope John Paul II. This is the real work of the Church, not self-maintenance or even reconstruction, but evangelization.

17. William M. Shea, "Catholic Reaction to Fundamentalism," *Theological Studies* 57 (1996) 282–83.

Index of Names

Abelard, 36
Adam, Karl, 37, 38
Altham, Elizabeth, 1
Angelica, Mother, 6, 7, 96
Anselm, ix, 12
Appleby, R. Scott, 5
Aquinas, Thomas, 12, 28, 36, 38, 57, 74
Aristides, 36
Athenagoras, 36
Augustine, 111

Balasuriya, Tissa, 18
Balthasar, Hans Urs von, 38
Barmejo, Luis, 45, 64
Barth, Karl, 35
Beaudoin, Tom, 107
Bellah, Robert, 108
Belloc, Hilaire, 37, 43
Benson, Robert Hugh, 37, 38
Bernardin, Joseph, 8, 116
Bertone, Tarcisio, 68
Blaire, Stephen, 51
Bloesch, Donald, 109–110
Blondel, Maurice, 37, 38
Boff, Leonardo, 18
Boniface VIII, Pope, 63
Borg, Marcus, 26

Bracken, Joseph, 22
Brown, Raymond E., 5, 9, 23, 27, 58, 60

Cahill, Lisa, 77, 78
Callan, James, 2
Carey, Patrick, 3, 15
Castillo, Jose María, 18
Chardin, Teilhard de, 14, 38
Chenu, Marie-Dominque, 14
Chesterton, Gilbert Keith, 37, 38, 42, 43
Chopra, Deepak, 107
Christ, Carol, 21
Chrysostom, John, 38
Clark, Matthew, 2
Clement of Alexandria, 36, 38
Collins, Raymond, 79
Congar, Yves, 13, 24
Cooke, Bernard, 14
Copernicus, ix
Crossan, John Dominic, 26–27
Cuneo, Michael, 5
Currie, David, 39
Curran, Charles, 16, 18, 73, 74, 76

Daly, Mary, 20
Daniélou, Jean, vii
Davidson, James, 71–72

Dawson, Christopher, 37
Deck, Allan Figueroa, 48–49, 114
Dierks, Sheila Durkin, 31
Dionne, J. Robert, 64
Downey, Michael, 107
Drey, Johann von, 36
Dulles, Avery, 5, 11, 13, 31, 32, 35, 37, 54–55, 99, 105, 114
Dupuis, Jacques, 18

Erlich, Johann, 36
Estrada, Juan, 18
Eusebius, 336

Fessio, Joseph, 7
Fiedler, Maureen, 45, 64
Fiorenza, Francis Schüssler, 37
Fitzmyer, Joseph, 59, 60
Forcano, Benjamin, 18
Ford, John C., 45
Fournier, Keith, 39
Fox, Matthew, 18
Fuchs, Josef, 76
Funk, Robert, 25
Furnish, Victor, 75

Galileo, ix
Gebara, Ivone, 18
Genovesi, Vincent, 75
George, Timothy, 4, 69
Grandmaison, Léonce de, 37
Greeley, Andrew, 71, 80, 82, 115
Grisez, Germain, 45
Guitton Jean, 37

Hahn, Kimberly, 39, 40
Hahn, Scott, 35, 39–41, 42, 43, 114
Haight, Roger, 102
Häring, Bernard, 76
Hayes, Richard, 27
Heidegger, Martin, 38
Hick, John, 24, 108
Hitchcock, Hellen Hull, 5
Hitchcock, James, 5
Holmberg, Bengt, 30

Hoose, Bernard, 73
Howard, Thomas, 35, 39
Howell, Kenneth, 41
Huff, Peter, 39, 43, 51

Ignatius of Antioch, 117

John Paul II, Pope, ix, 28, 29, 35, 50, 51, 66, 73, 75, 82, 99–102, 113, 119, 120, 126
John XXIII, Pope, 63
Johnson, Elizabeth, 21, 118
Johnson, Luke Timothy, 25, 27, 122
Jones, E. Michael, 6
Jungmann, Joseph, 89–90

Kasper, Walter, 23, 46
Kean, Philip, 77
Keating, Karl, 6, 35, 39, 40, 41, 44–46, 48–49
Kelly, George A., 5
Kerkhofs, Jan, 100
King, Eleace, 49
Klein, Leo, 93
Knauer, Peter, 73
Knitter, Paul, 24, 108
Knox, Ronald, 37, 38, 43
Komonchak, Joseph, 45
Kreeft, Peter, 35, 39, 42, 46, 50, 102–103
Küng, Hans, 16, 18, 39, 108

LaCugna, Catherine, 18–19
Lewis, C. S., 37, 42
Lindsell, Harold, 57
Lindsey, Hal, 69
Lonergan, Bernard, 12
Lubac, Henri de, vii, 14, 96
Lunn, Arnold, 37, 38

Macy, Gary, 31
Madrid, Patrick, 35, 39
Madox, Randy, 103
Maguire, Frank, 8
Mahoney, John, 80
Mahony, Roger, 7, 8, 96

Marsden, George, 43–44, 104
Marty, Martin, 57
Martyr, Justin, 36, 38
Matatics, Gerry, 39
Mayeski, Marie Anne, 28
McBrien, Richard, 4, 68
McCormick, Richard, 72
McFague, Sallie, 21–22
McGuire, Meredith, 108
McNeil, John, 76
McPartlan, Paul, 96
Meier, John P., 9, 23, 46
Mello, Anthony de, 18
Metz, Johann Baptist, 112–113
Moore, Thomas, 107
Morris, Charles, 82, 115
Most, William, 40
Mouw, Richard, 109
Murray, John Courtney, 6, 14
Myers, David, 81

Neuhaus, Richard John, 6
Newman, John Henry, 13, 36
Nichols, Terence, 29
Noll, Mark, 44, 104
Norris, Kathleen, 56
Novak, Michael, 5, 6, 122

O'Collins, Gerald, 39
O'Meara, Thomas, 14
O'Neill, Dan, 40
Origen, 36
Örsy, Ladislas, 67

Pacwa, Mitch, 39
Pascal, Blaise, 38
Paul III, Pope, 13
Paul IV, Pope, 13
Paul VI, Pope, vii, 5, 35, 51, 60, 63,
    65, 67–68, 99–100
Peck, Scott, 107
Pelikan, Jaroslav, 19
Pius IX, Pope, 64
Pius X, Pope, 13
Pius XII, Pope, ix, 13, 14, 59, 64

Quinn, John, 29–30, 42–43

Rahner, Karl, 14, 38, 39, 118
Ratzinger, Joseph, 8, 39, 67, 68
Rausch, Thomas, 30
Read, William, 50
Reese, Thomas, 71
Reiff, Philip, 1–6, 107
Rogers, Jack, 116
Roof, Wade Clark, 107
Ruether, Rosemary, 27

Sawicki, Marianne, 23
Schaberg, Jane, 23
Scheler, 38
Schillebeeckx, Edward, 18, 23, 31, 60
Schlette, Heinz, 108
Schneiders, Sandra, 31
Schreiter, Robert, 47
Schüssler Fiorenza, Elisabeth, 24–25,
    28, 30, 76–77
Scopes, John, 120
Seinfels, Peter, 28, 31
Shalit, Wendy, 82
Shea, Mark, 35, 39
Shea, William, 49, 50, 126
Sheed, Frank, 37
Snyder, Graydon, 9
Stebbins, H. Lyman, 5
Sullivan, Francis A., 66, 67, 74
Swaggart, Jimmy, 45

Tacelli, Ronald, 39, 42
Tertullian, 36, 38
Thielicke, Helmut, 81–82
Tracy, David, 118
Tripole, Martin, 103

Untener, Kenneth, 8

Vanauken, Sheldon, 35, 39
Vree, Dale, 8, 39

Weakland, Rembert, 7, 67, 71, 88,
    94–95, 98, 115–116

Weaver, Mary Jo, 5
Weigel, George, 6
Weinandy, Thomas, 106
Williams, D. H., 54, 69

Wister, Robert, 37
Wolff, Madeleva, 14
Wood, Steve and Karen, 39

Index of Subjects

"Always Our Children," 7
America, 8
Analogy, analogical language, 118
Anglicanism, 117
Anti-Semitism, 38
Apologetics, 35–39, 122
Apologists, new, 6, 39–48, 50–52
Apostolic ministry, 121
Association of Catholic Colleges and
    Universities, 7
Authority, 29–31, 63–69, 113, 119,
    123

Baby Boomers, 107
Baltimore Catechism, 48
Baptism of desire, 111
Benediction, 94
Bible, biblical, 56–62, 69–70
    interpretation, 76–78, 117, 122
    morality, 76–80
    scholarship, criticism, 58–62
Biblicism, ix, 46, 104
Bishops, 126
Body of Christ, 92, 95

Call to Action, 3
Calvinism, 104, 117
Canon Law Society, 7

CARA, 49
Catechism of the Catholic Church, 75,
    116, 117–118
Catholic, Catholicism, 117–119
    the Catholic middle, 115–116
Catholic Answers, 6
Catholic Theological Society of
    America, 7, 15, 31
Catholic World Report, 7
Catholics for Free Choice, 3
Catholics United for the Faith, 5, 7
Centesimus annus, 101
Christian Coalition, 105
Christology, 23–27, 104–109,
    109–110
Church, 32, 42, 62–70, 96, 105–106,
    110–111, 123
    as communion, 64, 110
    departures from, 48–50, 113
Classicist thinking, 12–14
Cohabitation, 81
College Theology Society, 3
Colleges and universities, Catholic, 3,
    4, 15–16, 32, 37, 59, 102–103, 114,
    126
    conservative colleges, 6, 39, 40, 42
Coming Home Network, 41
"Common Ground," 8, 125–126

Common Sense, 44, 97, 120
Conciliarism, 63
Confession, private, 63
Congregation for the Doctrine of the
    Faith, 16, 65–68, 121
Conscience, 83
Constitution on the Sacred Liturgy,
    91–93
Conversion, 112–113
Converts, 39–40, 51, 113
Corpus, 3
Crucifix, 89
Culture, dialogue with, 38–39, 51,
    101, 105, 108, 113–114
Curia, Roman, 29

Dei Verbum, 55–56, 58, 59, 62, 122
Dignity, 3
Discipleship, 79–80, 113
Divino Afflante Spiritu, 14, 59
Dissent, 11, 68, 71
Divorce, 81, 84, 119
Doctrine, 62–69, 112, 124
    and Catholics, 71–72
    and dogma, 65
    development of, 45, 62–65, 111,
        112, 121, 123
    historically conditioned, 121

Ecclesia in America, 50, 101
Ecumenism, 101, 105–106, 124
Eternal Word Television Network, 6,
    7, 39, 42
Eucharist, 46, 87–98
    eucharistic presidency, 31–32, 88,
        95
Evangelicals, 19, 48, 49, 57, 101,
    104–105, 109, 111, 113, 117, 124
Evangelii nuntiandi, 99–100
Evangelium vitae, 67
Evangelization, 4, 35, 49–50, 99–114,
    126
    new, 100–102
Evolution, 120
Ex Corde Ecclesiae, 16

Faith, 122
Faith and reason, vii–ix, 12, 51–52,
    113, 114, 119–120
Family values, 105
Fellowship of Catholic Scholars, 5
Feminist scholarship, 19, 20–21,
    24–25, 29, 30
Fidelity, 6
Fideism, ix
Fides et Ratio, ix, 119–120
Focus on the Family, 105
Fundamentalism, 48–49, 60–61, 104,
    113, 114, 117, 126
    Catholic, 5, 42–43, 51, 113

Generation X, 107
God, 20–22, 118
Goddess, 21
Gordon-Conwell, 41
Gospel, 59, 80–84, 99, 102, 114, 126

Haec sancta, 63
Heresy, 117
Hierarchy, 29, 125
    of truths, 124
Hispanic Catholicism, 49–50
Historical Consciousness, 12–14,
    121–122
Historical Critical Method, 60–62, 122
Holy Office, 13
Home schooling, 6
Homosexuality, 74–76, 83
Humani generis, ix, 13
Humanae vitae, 5, 45, 63

Inclusive language, 1, 7, 93, 115
Inculturation, 92, 119
Index of Forbidden Books, 13
Inerrancy, 57–58, 60, 61, 69
Infallible definitions, 64, 66–69, 74
"Instruction on the Ecclesial Vocation
    of the Theologian," 66
"Instruction on the Historical Truth of
    the Gospels," 59
Integralism, 42–43

Internet, vii–viii, 6, 7
Interpretation, biblical, 76–78
    private, 69
*Interpretation of the Bible in the
    Church,* 44–45, 61–62, 122

Jesus, historical, 60
Jesus Seminar, 25–27, 77
Justification, 112

Lamentabili, 13
Lay preaching, presiding, 88, 97
Liberation theologies, 3, 30, 106–107
Literary forms, 57
Liturgy, 87–93
    liturgical assembly, 89, 91–92, 95
    liturgical ministries, 92, 93
    liturgical music, 93–94
Lutheranism, 117

Magisterium, 19, 45, 61, 62, 67–68,
    70, 84, 112, 121, 123
Marquette University, 14–15
Mass, 91, 97
    attendance at, 100
    Tridentine, 119
Mediator Dei, 14
Ministry, 31–32
Miracles, 23, 46–47
Modernism, 13, 37, 46
Moral Majority, 105
Moral theology, 72–76
    and the magisterium, 74
    traditionalist vs revisionist, 73
Mulieris dignitatem, 28
Mysterium ecclesiae, 16, 121
Mystici Corporis, 14

National Coalition of American Nuns,
    3
Natural law, 72–73, 80, 84
Neoconservatives, 6
New Oxford Review, 7–8, 39, 41
Non-historical orthodoxy, 5, 45, 122

Ontologism, ix
Opus Dei, 2
Ordinatio sacerdotalis, 66–67
Original sin, 111
Our Sunday Visitor, 8

Pascendi, 13
Pentecostals, 48–50
Philosophy, 15, 120
Pontifical Biblical Commission,
    58–62, 122
Postmodernism, 44, 106, 113
Poverty, the poor, 101, 106, 114
Presbyterian Church, 116
Priesthood, 90
Priests for Equality, 3
Primacy, papal, 29, 45, 62–63, 121
"Profession of Faith," 65–66
Proportionalism, 72–74
Proselytism, 48
Protestant churches, 116, 117

Rationalism, ix
RCIA, 113
Real presence, 90, 94, 95, 96–97
Reception, 45, 63–64, 123
Redemption, 110
Redemptoris missio, 4, 100, 123
Religious education, 47–48
Religious studies, 15, 123
Resurrection, 23, 47
Revelation, 55–56, 58, 118
    two source theory, 55, 122
Roman Catholic Faithful, 7

Salvation, 102–103, 103–109
    outside the Church, 111
Science and theology, 119–120
Scripture, 56–62, 69–70
    Catholic Church and, 58–62, 70
Sectarianism, sects, 117, 118, 121
Seminaries, 47–48
Sensus fidelium, 63, 123
Sexuality, sexual morality, 71–85
    and Scripture, 76–80, 84
Sheilaism, 108

Social justice, 99–100, 103, 105, 113
Sojourners, 105
Sola Scriptura, 54, 69
Spirit, 123
Spirituality, 107–108
St. Joseph Communication, 41
Steubenville, Franciscan University of, 6, 41, 42
"Sunday Worship in the Absence of a Priest," 88
Synod of Bishops, 29, 99

Theologians censured, 18
Theological language, 118–119
Theology, 11–33, 42, 51–52, 102–109, 114, 117–126
    and apologetics, 36–39
    and Church, 32–33
    evangelical, 109–114, 123–124
    feminist, 19, 20–21, 24–25, 29
    fundamental, 37, 120
    laicization of, 14–15
    nouvelle théologie, 14
    of complementarity, 28, 81
    Roman, 13, 37
Therapeutic, the, 107–108
"To Defend the Faith," 68
Tradition, 19, 48, 54–56, 62, 69–70, 112

Traditionalism, 19
Transubstantiation, 90, 96
Trent, Council of, 55
Trinity, 22
Truth, 117, 120, 124
    double truth, 12, 120
Tübingen School, 13, 36
Twelve, the, 29, 30

Unam sanctam, 63
Ut unum sint, 29, 101

Vatican I, 29, 121
Vatican II, 2, 12, 47, 68, 122
    and liturgy, 90–93
    and moral theology, 76
Veritatis splendor, 73, 74, 75
Veterum sapientiae, 63

Wanderer, The, 5, 7
We Are the Church, 3
Women for Faith and Family, 6
Women in the Church, 27–28, 119
    ordination of, 29, 63, 65–67
Women's Ordination Conference, 3, 28
World religions, 108–109
World Vision, 105